MODERN THEOLOGY

3. Paul Tillich

MODERN THEOLOGY

Selections from twentieth-century theologians
edited with an introduction and notes by

E. J. TINSLEY

3

Paul Tillich

1886–1965

LONDON

EPWORTH PRESS

Enquiries should be addressed to
The Methodist Publishing House
The Book Room
2 Chester House
Muswell Hill
London N10 1PZ

SBN 7162 0217 4

Printed in Great Britain by
The Garden City Press Limited
Letchworth, Hertfordshire
SG6 1JS

ACKNOWLEDGEMENTS

The author and publisher are grateful for permission to quote in this series from the following works:

Church Dogmatics, Vol. I, 2; IV, 2, T. and T. Clark
Deliverance to the Captives, by Karl Barth, SCM Press
Kerygma and Myth, Vol. I; II, edited by H. W. Bartsch, SPCK
Christology, by Dietrich Bonhoeffer, Collins Publishers
Ethics, by Dietrich Bonhoeffer, SCM Press
Letters and Papers from Prison, by Dietrich Bonhoeffer, SCM Press
Sanctorum Communio, by Dietrich Bonhoeffer, Collins Publishers
The Cost of Discipleship, by Dietrich Bonhoeffer, SCM Press
Form Criticism, by Bultmann and Kundsin, Harper and Row, New York
Theology of the New Testament, Vol. II, by Rudolf Bultmann, translated by F. Grobel, SCM Press
Word and Faith, by G. Ebeling, translated by J. W. Leitch, SCM Press
The Nature of Faith, by Gerhard Ebeling, Collins Publishers
Selections from Karl Barth's Church Dogmatics, by H. Gollwitzer, T. and T. Clark
The Systematic Theology of Paul Tillich, by A. J. McKelway, Lutterworth Press
Beyond Tragedy, by Reinhold Niebuhr, James Nisbet and Co. Ltd
Leaves from the Notebook of a Tamed Cynic, by Reinhold Niebuhr, Harper and Row, New York
The Nature and Destiny of Man, Vol. I; II, by Reinhold Niebuhr, James Nisbet and Co. Ltd
World Come of Age, edited by R. Gregor Smith, Collins Publishers
The Death of God, by Gabriel Vahanian, George Braziller, Inc., New York

CONTENTS

PREFACE TO THE SERIES

The theologians represented in this series of five volumes of selections are those who, one can confidently say, are already assured of an important place in the history of twentieth-century theology.

In the case of each theologian I have tried to give a fair representation of the author's work although, inevitably, there are important aspects of his thought which I have not always found it possible to illustrate. I have throughout preferred to give substantial selections rather than short extracts because the qualities of the writing of the theologians in this collection require this treatment for proper understanding and illustration. Even so selections are no substitute for the original, and it is my hope that readers will become sufficiently interested in what is given in this series to want to go to the full range of the authors' complete works.

As well as being representative of an influential group of theologians I hope that the selections provided will be found to provide something of an integrated discussion among the writers themselves. I have, therefore, in making the selections included some which give an idea how these theologians view each other. The reader is given some indication of the views, say, of Barth on Bultmann or Niebuhr on Barth, and there are cross-references in the introduction and notes so that he can have an idea of what subjects have been of continuing importance in modern theological discussion.

I have made this selection not only for those who have a professional interest in the study of theology (clergy and ministers, teachers, students) but also for the interested member of the general public who, whether believer or not, wishes to have a guide to a reading of some important phases of twentieth-century theology. A general introduction attempts to set the scene and for each author there is a biographical note and brief introductions to the selected passages. In each case also there are suggestions for further study and reading.

University of Leeds   JOHN TINSLEY

INTRODUCTION TO THE SERIES

In this introductory chapter an attempt will be made to explain how the present theological situation in western Europe and the United States has come about. We shall trace very briefly the pedigree of contemporary ideas and attitudes. 'Theology' however is a word (like, e.g., 'mysticism', 'romanticism', 'philosophy') which is frequently and easily used without its meaning having first been made clear. It is not uncommon to find politicians and other public speakers using the word 'theology' to mean some recondite, antiquarian and hopelessly irrelevant intellectual pursuit involving, it is implied, a sad waste of mental energy. It is essential therefore to try first to clarify the meaning of the term 'theology'. A good way of doing this is to describe how theology is done. By describing the process of theology we shall more easily come to an understanding of what it essentially is.

Perhaps there have been as many attempts at a definition of theology as, for example, of art. The comparison with art is very relevant because theology is in one aspect, and a very important one, an instance of the perennial task of working with words to achieve lucidity and precision described by T. S. Eliot as 'the intolerable wrestle with words and meanings'. Even if we think we have found a more or less satisfactory language very often the cultural situation will have meantime so moved on that we find, in Eliot's words again, that we have only learned to get better words for the things we no longer want to say.

Nevertheless theologians have to keep on with this task not because they believe that it is possible, for instance, to describe 'God' or to find a language about God which is valid for all time, but because they believe that theology is a perennial human task. Man is a 'theologizing' animal: i.e., he must be constantly attempting to achieve in a significant pattern of words (or of words together with gestures and sound, as, for example, in liturgy) some way of rationalizing all those facets of his experience and history which point to a meaning beyond the visible and material. Because the most significant activity in religion, worship, involves among other things a particular use of language theology is, whether the fact be acknowledged by theologians or not, vitally linked with the arts and the problems raised by artistic creativity. Hence the amount of space taken up in this book with discussion of the nature of religious language, and the use of symbol, myth and metaphor in religion.

These subjects are of common interest to theologians and students of literature, and of the arts in general. The question of theology and language is however of special concern to the *Christian* theologian and the reason for this has never been better expressed than by St Augustine. In a famous passage in his *De Trinitate* he discusses the question why Christians should use trinitarian language when speaking about God. He is aware of the irritation and impatience of those who feel that theological language is attempting to make definitions precisely in a sphere where, in the nature of the case, such a thing is not possible. Augustine replies, however, that Christians have to be careful about language, especially language about God, *non ut diceretur sed ne taceretur*, which could be paraphrased 'not in order to define but because it is not possible just to say nothing'. Christians, of all people, cannot keep silence, adds Augustine, because God has broken silence in Christ and has spoken to mankind in him. We are bound therefore to make the best reply that we can.

More particularly theology invites comparison with what may properly be called the art of criticism, since it has the same relation to its subject matter (religion) as, for example, music criticism has to the symphony, art criticism to painting or sculpture, or literary criticism to poetry or prose. The best theology, like the best art, is that which so uses language that it sends the reader back with new and fruitful perspectives to the original (e.g., Christ, the Bible, etc.), or so speaks of the original that it affords a fresh and creative present experience of it.

Perhaps because of the great variety of approaches and methods possible for doing theology it is better, and here again the analogy from art is useful, not to think of what theology may be in the abstract but of actual types and styles of theology, and it is hoped that the selections given in this book will enable the reader to do this. The types and styles of theology are analogous to the types and styles of art. One could readily think in theology of the equivalents of, say, representational, impressionist, expressionist or abstract art. The 'quest of the historical Jesus' in the nineteenth century bears a resemblance to the 'pre-Raphaelite' school of painting in its attempt to portray Jesus in full and minute detail. Rudolf Bultmann and the 'existentialist' school of modern theology remind one of German 'expressionist' art where the subject of the painting is used as a means of expressing the commitment, feeling and attitudes of the artist. Further, like styles in art, theological styles continue to have significance even though they belong to an age now long past. The artist and the theologian are both in constant dialogue with their past traditions. To be a genuine contemporary, in both fields, means to have lived through, in imaginative experience, the outlook of previous practitioners. Theology belongs to the realm of human creativity and is therefore a dynamic and changing phenomenon. It is better, therefore, at the beginning of one's study of such a subject to look at the various methods of doing theology rather than to seek some distillation of it, some quintessential theology.

It would not be difficult to say something about what theology is from an analysis of the two words which make up the term theology—'theos' and 'logos'. Starting from these two components we might translate 'theology' as 'God-talk'. Theology as 'God-talk' takes its origin from two permanent features of human existence. There is first the fact that from time to time, in all sorts of ways, man finds himself wondering whether there is any meaning to his existence, whether the values and ideals which strike him in a cogent way in his many moral and aesthetic experiences are anything more than fine moments of feeling. There is further an impatience and a restlessness about human existence—we long for serenity, for wholeness and harmony, for unity and purpose, and continue to wonder whether in and behind material existence there is another order of reality.

These intimations of something beyond time and space have been variously expressed whether in the classical scheme of the values of 'truth, beauty and goodness', or in what Rudolf

Otto[1] has called the experience of the 'holy' or the 'numinous', or as far as aesthetic experience is concerned, in what Longinus[2] called the 'sublime'. Others have used the term 'mystery' for these features of human existence to express their sense of that which is mysterious, not in the way of a puzzle which is in principle solvable at some time or other, but as inducing, rather than the desire to solve, an overwhelming impression of awe, wonder, reverence, joy.

For the centre of this 'mystery' the Greek word would have been *theos,* sometimes translated 'god', but we may conveniently use it for any kind of transcendental reference given to human life. Man is a being who finds it difficult to undergo artistic, religious, scientific or moral experience and leave it just like that. He finds himself involved necessarily in the task of shaping this experience into significant patterns, trying to hold it in words or in some visual form. More particularly he is prompted to speech about it, to try and contain this experience in sentences. It is to this necessary use of language to analyse and explain *theos* that one can give the Greek word *logos.* Theology is, therefore, strictly speaking *theos-logos*—'God-talk'. Theology results from the fact that on the one hand there is the 'mystery' and on the other the impulse to achieve understanding of it.

It is significant that many theologians have expressed a similar impatience with their task to that which we find in poets. We have already referred to Augustine and T. S. Eliot on the difficulties and frustrations of finding satisfactory words. This raises an important issue. Most frequently when we use the term 'theology' we think, inevitably and rightly, of verbal theology: that analysis of the 'mystery' of existence, that articulation of *theos* which can be done in words (*logos*). No doubt one would have to say that the best theology is that which approximates most closely to the character of its subject-matter. In the case of Christian theology this would mean the character of the Incarnation especially its 'signful', indirect, ambiguous, parabolic quality. Perhaps a more adequate kind of theology, a more satisfactory response to the *theos,* is that

[1] *The Idea of the Holy,* 1923.
[2] Cassius Longinus, Greek philosopher and critic of third century A.D., author of a treatise on literary criticism, *On the sublime.*

expressed in a concrete but non-verbal way in the arts, particularly the visual arts. If this is the case we ought to coin a new word for this reaction to *theos*. It would be a question not of *theos* and *logos* (=*verbal* theology) but of *theos* and *poiesis* ('making')—'theo-poetics'. The use of such a term as 'theo-poetics' would remind one of the saying of W. B. Yeats, specially appropriate to the Christian religion, that man cannot know the truth or express it in words. He can only *embody* (perhaps one could say 'incarnate') it. Even if we must continue to use the word 'theology' we need to think of it as a perennial attempt to *embody* human experience of *theos* rather than to translate it into some prose paraphrase.

This analysis of the meaning of the word 'theology' is a start, but it does not take us very far. We need to examine more closely how theologians have set about the task of 'God-talk', and the data which they have taken to be relevant. We must therefore turn now to a brief re-view of what theologians have been doing during the last two centuries. This will help us to understand the theological scene today, and to recognize more clearly some of the 'styles' being used by theologians at the present time.

1

A radical change came over the method of doing Christian theology in the eighteenth century. Up till then, broadly speaking, and certainly from the time when theology had been given its most comprehensive and systematic expression in the works of St Thomas Aquinas (*c.* 1225–74) the procedure had seemed straightforward and uncomplicated. The scheme of theological investigation had two main parts: (1) natural theology and (2) revealed theology.

To take the method of doing 'natural' theology first. It was thought possible to establish by the ordinary processes of human reasoning such great truths as the existence of God and the immortality of the soul. Furthermore the ordinary processes of argumentation could establish the truth of certain attributes of God, like his omnipotence and omnipresence. From the evidence provided by the natural world and human existence it was possible to establish the existence of God by 'proofs'. The existence of God could be demonstrated by the use of unaided human reason. This was a truth about God open to any enquirer and could therefore rightly be called 'natural' theology.

'Revealed' theology was an important supplement to this. It had two additional functions to those performed by natural theology. First of all it conveyed again the truths of natural theology but this time in a 'revealed' form (particularly in the Christian scriptures) which could be readily and easily understood by those who were not able to follow rational argument. Then, second, revealed theology presented truths which could not be demonstrated by human reason, such as, for instance, the trinitarian nature of God. The scriptures attested the divinity of Christ by showing that he fulfilled Old Testament prophecy and worked miracles. These were taken to be the two foundations of belief in the authority of Christ. They established his place in the Christian revelation.

There were thus two kinds of data at the disposal of the theologian, natural theology and revealed theology, or to put it shortly 'reason' and 'revelation'. From an investigation of the book of nature and the book of scripture the theologian could construct an integrated and systematic theology, like the *Summa Theologiae* of St Thomas Aquinas. This was the general pattern of Christian apologetics commonly accepted until comparatively recently, and has remained the official view of the matter in the Roman Catholic Church. This method of doing theology was enshrined in William Paley's *View of the Evidences of Christianity* (1794) which remained in use as a text-book until as late as the beginning of the present century. Various criticisms had been brought against this way of doing theology before the advent of modern developments in philosophy, the sciences, and in biblical criticism. Reformation theology in general was suspicious of the large claims made by natural theology for the use of man's 'unaided' reason. Not only did the Reformers insist on the fact that all reasoning is undergirded by grace but they questioned whether one could say that human reason, even when so supported, inevitably attained the truths of natural theology. This seemed to them to neglect the problem of 'fallen' human nature which is capable of perverting and corrupting even the process of reasoning. During the eighteenth century the unsatisfactory character of this traditional approach to theology became clearer still. Many Christian apologists in this period tried to develop a natural theology not by reading off from the book of nature but by searching, so to speak, the book of man's inner experience. This seemed to show that there was among human beings a general religious sense which lay behind all formally organized religions. So-called 'revealed' theology was therefore taken to be simply a sophisticated articulation of this universal natural theology. In this way the distinction between natural and revealed theology was blurred, to say the least. Christianity, for example, was seen not as a blend of natural and revealed theology but a particular version of the universal feeling for religion. To quote from the title of a book by a famous eighteenth-century Deist, Matthew Tindal, it was as 'old as creation', nothing more than 'a republication of the religion of nature'.

More dramatic in their effects on the traditional scheme of theology, however, were the developments in scientific investigation and historical criticism which gathered momentum during the eighteenth century and continued apace throughout the nineteenth century.

2

Research in the natural sciences during the nineteenth century, especially in the fields of geology and biology, produced a picture of the origin of the universe and its evolution radically different from that suggested by a literal acceptance of the early chapters of Genesis with a universe created in six days and an Adam and Eve as the first human beings. *The Bridgewater Treatises* (1833–40) showed, among other things, that it was quite impossible, from the evidence already made available by geological research, to subscribe to the view that Creation could be exactly dated, as Archbishop Ussher[1] had

---

[1] James Ussher (1581–1656), Archbishop of Armagh, worked out a complete biblical chronology in his *Annales Veteris et Novi Testamenti*, and the dates given in this book were inserted in editions of the Authorised Version of the Bible from 1701 onwards.

suggested, in 4004 B.C. For those who had been brought up on the idea that the Bible was itself the revelation of God, giving infallible truth as a series of propositions, this suggestion that the earth was millions rather than thousands of years old came as quite a shock. As late as 1851 John Ruskin could write: 'If only the geologists would let me alone, I could do very well, but those dreadful hammers! I hear the clink of them at the end of every cadence of the Bible verses.'

Following hard upon this shock came the news from the field of biological research. Charles Darwin's *The Origin of Species* was published in 1859 and his *The Descent of Man* in 1871. These made it clear not only that human life had evolved from sub-human species but that the whole process had been inconceivably longer than was generally supposed. Again for those brought up on the view that the Bible was a monolithic structure infallible on all subjects, including the science of human origins, this came as a great blow.

These shocks from outside the sphere of the Bible coincided with developments within biblical criticism which at the time seemed to undermine still further the status of the Bible as authoritative Scripture. As a result of literary and historical study it was no longer possible to maintain that the biblical literature was all of one kind, and all on the same level of authority or 'inspiration'. To take the Bible as an infallible oracle, to believe that in it the Word of God took print, was now seen to violate the nature of the biblical literature itself and to presuppose that the divine method of revelation is one which imposes rather than elicits, 'explains' rather than indicates, and forces rather than persuades.

Faced with these developments there were three possible reactions from Christian apologists. One could first simply refuse to recognize that any change had taken place and to carry on using the Bible as before, if anything hardening one's ideas about its authority and inerrancy. This is the approach which later on came to have the label 'fundamentalism' attached to it. Or, secondly, the attempt could be made to reconcile the new developments in knowledge with the traditional structure of theology. This was often taken to quite fantastic lengths like, for example, suggesting that the real significance of fossils in no way turned out to be a contradiction of the traditional dating of creation since they had been placed there by God to test faith! Similarly one remembers the notorious attempts to reconcile evolution with the scheme of creation in Genesis. Since the psalmist says that one day in the sight of the Lord is as a thousand years, 'days' in the Genesis account does not mean twenty-four hours but whatever extended period of time may be necessary to fit the case! Or, thirdly, one could accept the findings of research and in the light of them discard previous views of, for example, biblical inerrancy and look entirely afresh at the whole concept of revelation and the nature of the biblical literature. It was this latter reaction that has come to be known as nineteenth-century liberalism. Its main features were as follows.

First, a suspicion of the traditional schemes of dogmatic theology, and an attempt to reconstruct Christian belief in a way which took into account historical criticism. This could be illustrated by new procedures in such areas as christology or the doctrine of the Church. The traditional belief about the Christ as true God and true man, with two natures divine and human, as expressed in the traditional formula of the Council of Chalcedon 451 was put on one side, and an attempt made to construct a way of believing in Christ taking into account the results of historical criticism of the gospels, particularly the growing conviction that the fourth gospel, which had been a principal source for the formulation of traditional christology, was so much later than the synoptic gospels and so much less historical that it ought not to be used again in this way. The enigmatical Christ of the synoptic gospels, only indirectly indicating the meaning of himself, became the basis for a 'kenotic' christology. That is to say it was emphasized that whatever else the Incarnation was it meant an act of self-giving on the part of God which involved sacrificial self-limitation. Or again one could take the doctrine of the Church, especially in its relation to Christ. In the light of biblical and historical criticism it was felt by many nineteenth-century scholars that the Christ of history, the genuine Jesus of Nazareth, was one thing, and the Christ of Church doctrine quite another. It seemed to be self-evident that the historical Christ could not have intended the Church as an institution, but rather that he was an outstanding Hebrew prophet who was concerned with brotherly love, justice, and the inestimable worth of the human soul.

The second characteristic of nineteenth-century liberalism was the use made of the category of evolution, provided by developments in the biological sciences. Human history was seen in terms of evolutionary progress. Mankind was seen to be, indubitably, on the march of progress. By the use of reason and the intellectual tools at his disposal man would be able to fashion a better future for himself. 'Sin', if the word were used at all, ought to be put in inverted commas and translated to mean imperfection or ignorance. 'Salvation' consequently ought to be thought of in terms of education and enlightenment. Such biblical concepts as 'the kingdom of God' ought similarly to be reinterpreted in terms of some kind of evolutionary progressivism.

Out of all this came some new principles for theological method and the data to be used by theology. The Bible remained as a principal source for the Christian theologian but it had to be used critically in the light of the findings of literary and historical investigation. The Bible also needed to be detached from its traditional interpretation in the church. In particular allegorization and typology were discarded as both inappropriate and irrelevant to such a critical use of the Bible. The book of the universe, nature, was also a source to be used, especially since it provided such a category of interpretation as evolutionary development. Finally there was increasing use of human experience as a source for theology. Nineteenth-century theology was greatly influenced by the work of Friedrich Schleiermacher (1768–1834) who considered the essence of the religious sentiment to be the feeling of absolute dependence and interpreted Christ as the supreme example of such dependence and 'God-consciousness'.

As far as relations with philosophy were concerned it has to be remembered that in the nineteenth century the task of philosophy was taken to be, principally, to provide a 'metaphysics', that is an all-embracing interpretation of the universe and human existence. The philosopher was one who concerned himself with what Tillich (see pp. 73 ff.) called the 'ultimate questions of human existence'. The theologian's task was to keep on the look-out for philosophical schemes whose general outlook and vocabulary seemed to be particularly well-suited for the exposition of Christian beliefs. It was widely held during the nineteenth century, both on the Continent and in Britain, that such a congenial philosophical system had been found in the work of Friedrich Hegel (1770–1831). Hegel believed that existence could best be interpreted in terms of an evolutionary process, continually advancing from thesis to antithesis and fresh synthesis, whereby the Absolute Idea realized itself in ever more sharply focused ways. Adapting Christian trinitarian language he thought of the eternal Idea as God the Father. The eternal Idea as constantly passing from infinitude to finitude he thought of as God the Son. The Absolute Idea returning home, so to speak, enriched by this outgoing (Incarnation) he identified with the Christian God the Holy Spirit.

3

This was the background against which we can place all the theological movements represented in this series. Paul Tillich has described himself as a nineteenth-century figure, and certainly his concept of the relation between theology and philosophy as a 'correlation' (see pp. 39 ff.) makes him very much more akin to the philosophy of the last century than to the analytical anti-metaphysical philosophy which has dominated the academic scene in twentieth-century Britain. Karl Barth's theological thinking began as a strong reaction against the liberal theology of the nineteenth-century and particularly its alliance with philosophies which he believed prevented the unique and distinctive features of the Christian religion from being clearly expressed. Bultmann took up the issues raised by the development of biblical criticism in the nineteenth century, particularly the question of the relation between the Jesus of history and the Christ of faith. Bonhoeffer in his early period shared Barth's reaction to nineteenth-century theology but later came to believe that a quite new situation faces the twentieth-century Christian and that Barth was of decreasing usefulness to such a person. Niebuhr's theology of politics and society is a deliberate reaction to a liberal theology which he believed had seriously underplayed the doctrines of sin and original sin and had placed an ultimate trust in human intelligence and virtue. We now need to examine more fully the place in the history of twentieth-century theology likely to be occupied by these five theologians.

All five of them were German or, in the case of Niebuhr, of German origin. As it happens they were also all of clerical or academic households. Further they all had experienced the age of Nazism and in most cases had suffered from it in one way or another.

The beginning of the theological movement associated with the name of *Karl Barth* can be dated from his shocked realization that the values of nineteenth-century liberalism as held by academics and intellectuals of his day left them incapable of recognizing tyranny when it appeared, much less of standing up against it. Academic education, even in theology, did not make men any more able to perceive the illiberalism and aggression implicit in the German policies which led to the outbreak of the 1914–18 war (see Vol. 1, pp. 36 ff.). The same inability of the liberal mind to believe in the recalcitrant and anti-rational possibilities of human conduct displayed itself again when the Nazis came to power in 1934. The theological charter which became the rallying point of church resistance to Hitler, the Barmen declaration, was mainly the work of Barth.

Certainly nothing could be more contrary to the theological method of nineteenth-century liberalism than that promulgated by Barth. For him the theological endeavour begins not with a series of questionings about human existence or the universe but by a realization that man is first confronted by an answer, a divine answer in the form of a revelation to which a unique witness is borne by the Bible. 'Religion' as the human enquiry after God, the human endeavour to attain God by the exercise of human reason is anathema to Barth (see Vol. 1, pp. 56 ff.). It is impossible for man to take any initiative, strictly speaking, in his enquiries about God because by his very existence man is a potential recipient of a relevation which is one of the inescapable givennesses of life. God is essentially a prevenient God who has first spoken to man, and anything that man says, any enquiry that he may make, must necessarily take the form of a response to a God who has all the while been addressing him. This is a method of doing theology directly opposed to that of Paul Tillich who begins his theology precisely with human questions, the 'ultimate questions' posed by human existence.

This starting point led Barth to place a new kind of emphasis on the Bible and the place of scripture in the formation of dogmatic theology. This started a movement which later on came to be known as 'biblical theology'. The Bible was regarded as providing the categories for Christian theology. Barth's theology has been given different names. One of them, his own term, is 'kerygmatic' theology, namely a theology which has first and foremost to be proclaimed. It is not sensible to argue about revelation Barth believed; one can only proclaim it.

There is also in Barth a new emphasis on the indissoluble links between theology and the church. Academic theology in the nineteenth century, especially in Germany, was separated from the life of the Church and the work of the pastor. The Church as the believing community came to have a new meaning for Barth as the body which finds itself bearing the Word of God and being judged by it.

Barth's way of doing Christology, of tackling the problems raised by the person of Christ, seems at first sight to be very much in the traditional manner. He began from the traditional formulation of the Council of Chalcedon of Christ as true God and true man. But he soon showed himself to be suspicious of the historical method of the nineteenth-century 'quest of the historical Jesus'. Barth suspected that this really made faith dependent on the results of historical investigation and practically equivalent to acceptance of an agreed amount of reliable factual information about Christ. It is instructive at this point to compare Barth's attitude to the historical Jesus with that of Bultmann, Tillich and Bonhoeffer. Barth treated more creatively and fruitfully than the nineteenth century the question of *kenosis* (self-emptying) in the Incarnation. This was not for Barth a matter of some loss of divinity, a downgrading of God. The *kenosis* in Christ is in fact the highest affirmation of the lordship of God over all. God is lord not only in transcendent glory but even in the form of the servant. God is free to be other personalities without ceasing to be himself. Whereas for so many 'kenotic' theologians in the nineteenth (and indeed twentieth centuries) the Incarnation had meant God revealing himself in a very qualified and impoverished way, for Barth the Incarnation is the expression (the Word) of a God who always had man, and the glorification of man, in mind. God in Christ revealed his majesty precisely in the humiliations, trials and sufferings of Christ which many theologians in the past had thought must conceal it.

The resulting shape of Barth's theological scheme gives central place to the Incarnation, Scripture, and the Church. All Christian theology turns out in the end, according to Barth, to be an aspect of Christology whether it be the doctrine of creation, or of the church, or of the sacraments.[1]

Barth may have been neo-Calvinist in his approach to the doctrine of man, emphasizing human impotence before God, but in the end his theology of man turns out to be more optimistic than, say, that of Tillich or Niebuhr. There is a warm glow about Barth's language when he writes about man as he is in Christ, re-created man. On the other hand his theology is distanced from cultural and social interests. Barth saw what he called a *diastasis,* a tension between theology and the arts where Tillich perceived the possibilities of 'correlation'.

For *Bultmann* too the 1914–18 war was a turning point. It was during this period that he was working as a New Testament scholar on the form-critical method (see Vol. 2, pp. 37 ff.) and this proved to be determinative for his later work. He was sceptical about being able to get behind the 'kerygmatic' Christ of the gospels and sure that we do not have data for providing informed discussion about such subjects as the motivation of Christ or the self-awareness about his own mission. As well as the influence of Bultmann's scholarly investigations we need to reckon with his deep interest in the problem of communication, and his concern with the pastoral problems created by the fact that the tradition about Jesus comes down to us in a 'mythological' form. The extent of this problem was brought home to him by what he heard from army chaplains in the Second World War about their experiences in trying to preach and teach. This raised in an acute form the whole

[1] *Church Dogmatics*, I, 2, pp. 123 ff.

question of how the Christian gospel is to be communicated in the modern world. This involved a study of the status of 'mythology' in the Christian religion. Is it an essential form of human speech, or it is accidental, temporary, continually replaceable by more satisfactory translations or paraphrases into other kinds of language? Bultmann came to believe the latter and hence insisted upon the need for 'demythologizing' (see Vol. 2, pp. 64 ff.).

Bultmann took over the language of 'existentialist' philosophy as that which is specially well equipped to express the kind of religious belief we find in the New Testament. 'Existentialist' thinking is that in which we are ourselves personally involved, the kind of thinking in which we are personally implicated. It calls for personal decision and genuine commitment. Existentialism is antipathetic to any philosophy which is merely theoretical or academic (in the bad sense). The debate started by Bultmann's transposition of New Testament belief into existentialist terms has centred on whether this emphasis on the subjective, on *my* decision and commitment here and now, is adequate to do justice to the many facets of Christianity. Is not the New Testament also concerned with certain objective facts, like the redemption wrought by Christ, which remain true irrespective of any personal decision and commitment. Sometimes after reading a lot of Bultmann one has the feeling that when the existentialist theologian says 'God' he really means 'me'. Or at least it sounds like that!

Bultmann shares the hesitations of Barth about exposing the Incarnation to the ambiguities and probabilities of historical investigation. This would make faith vulnerable to the hazards of historical criticism and Bultmann, like Barth, seems intent on finding some area for faith which is immune from that eventuality.

So the data for theology which is to determine one's starting point is not the world, nor is it the Bible in the way Barth takes it, although the New Testament plays a cardinal role in Bultmann's theology. Rather it is human existence, because this is where the whole question of faith is posed. The mythological idiom of the New Testament really relates to man in his existential predicaments, to the need for decision, and for turning from 'inauthentic' to 'authentic' existence.

When we turn to *Paul Tillich* we find a theologian who is very much closer than Barth or Bultmann to the liberal tradition and to principles of liberal investigation. Tillich's whole approach to theology is based on the assumption that man has a natural ability to apprehend truth and that there is in man 'a depth of reason'. He starts from anthropology, examining the implications of the questions which are set by human existence.

Tillich agreed with Barth that theology is 'kerygmatic' but he insisted that it is also 'apologetic'. He kept a place for 'natural theology'. If theology is treated as only 'kerygmatic' Tillich believed, and I think rightly, that it then becomes irrelevant outside the domestic circle of believers, and is only useful for 'revivalism', as he put it.

Tillich departed radically from Bultmann on the question of myth and symbol. 'Demythologizing' for Tillich was an impossible enterprise because the myth is by its very nature irreplaceable and untranslatable, and cannot be transposed into a paraphrase without serious distortion or reduction. 'Myth' is a significant pattern of symbols organized into a narrative story which has the peculiar power, whenever it is receptively read or heard of bringing with it a clearer perception and deeper understanding of some feature of human experience which can not be evoked or expressed in any other way. Tillich believed that myth was therefore fundamentally irreplaceable. Bultmann on the other hand does not see myth existing in its own permanent right, but rather as a temporary way of putting things in a certain culture, which may now be seen perhaps as striking and picturesque, but not a necessary form of human speech.

Tillich was outstanding among the group represented in this series, and indeed in the twentieth century generally, for the attention he gave to analysing the relation between theology and culture. On this issue he was far removed from Barth and closer to a thinker like Niebuhr.

Reinhold Niebuhr's work can also be seen as a reaction against the preceding liberal theology. He is specially critical of the tendencies in nineteenth-century theology to equate the 'kingdom of God' with social betterment or progress. His theological endeavour could be described as an essay in 'prophetic realism'. He sought, that is to say, to relate biblical insights into the meaning of history and God's judgement on and in it to the political and social situation of his day. His aim was 'realism' in the sense that he had a deep suspicion of what one American writer has called 'the men of the infinite', that is the idealists, the romantics, the men of abstract generalization. Niebuhr preferred the company of 'the men of the finite', those with a careful eye for data, evidence, facts. A good example of this 'prophetic realism' is to be found in the essay 'The ultimate trust' in *Beyond Tragedy*.

Like Tillich, but unlike Barth, Niebuhr starts from the human situation. Here again one finds his work a marked contrast to nineteenth-century liberalism in the way he expounds afresh the doctrines of the 'fall of man' and 'original sin', and the place he gives to eschatology. The basic form of sin for Niebuhr is not finitude or imperfection but the anxiety about them which human freedom makes possible and which expresses itself in pride and envy.

Niebuhr takes up from liberal theology the results of biblical criticism, especially as it affects biblical history. 'Fundamentalist' approaches to the Bible blurred the distinction between different literary forms, and, most disastrously, between symbolic language and language of historical fact.

The theology of *Bonhoeffer*, fragmentary though it be, is of the greatest importance in showing a man struggling to free himself from various traditions in his early training, notably the influence of Karl Barth, and re-cast the whole structure of theology to face a new situation. Bonhoeffer came to believe that the theology of Barth and Bultmann had seriously neglected the social and political problems of the world. In this respect he found the theology of Niebuhr, which he came to know well as a result of his visits to America, very much more congenial.

Bonhoeffer was very much concerned with the significance of Christ, and especially the place of the historical Christ in Christian belief. His theology is, in one respect, an attempt to reconstruct a Christocentric theology and ethics just as thoroughgoing in its Christocentricity as Barth's. He does not, however, isolate the place and role of the Bible in the manner of Barth nor does he put the whole stress on inwardness in the existentialist fashion of Bultmann and Tillich.

4

The theologians represented in this series are already established figures on the twentieth-century theological scene, and their writings have by now attained the status of 'classics'. What developments have there been among a younger genera- of theologians? Recently a number of new movements have come into vogue which could be given the labels: 'The new theology', 'Secular Christianity' and 'The death of God theology'. There is space here only for a brief word about each of these developments.

One of the most astonishing phenomena in recent years has been the popular success of Dr John A. T. Robinson's *Honest to God*, first published in 1963, which has now sold well over one million copies, as well as being translated into a great number of foreign languages. The extraordinary circulation of this book is strange because it was not written for a popular audience, it contains long extracts from Tillich, Bultmann and Bonhoeffer which make severe demands on the general reader, and it could not be described as a piece of creative or lucid theological writing. The author would be the first to say that he was not attempting a new theology but to promote a discussion of the three thinkers just mentioned who had hitherto, especially in this country, been known only by academics and professional theologians. It was perhaps the tone of voice of this book rather than its contents which gave it such popular appeal particularly since the author was a bishop, with all that the image of such a person still implies in this country. The picture which the book suggested of a bishop not pontificating theological certainties in dogmatizing fashion, but exploring in a very tentative way and voicing his own doubts and uncertainties, struck a new note for many people. *Honest to God* appeared to be the manifesto of a movement of liberation, and to express the feeling that belief was a continuous dialogue with doubt within each person, and not an unchangeable certainty over against the unbelief of others.

Many critics have pointed out the obscurities and confusions in Dr Robinson's book. One of these is significant and worth pausing over. This is the question of the place and function of metaphor in religious language which he brings up in the first chapter on the God 'up there or out there'. He expresses his irritation with this kind of language but without making it at all clear what he takes a phrase like 'God is up there' to mean. If he is arguing that God is not 'up there' in the sense that God is not an entity that one could theoretically examine in, say, the course of space exploration, this is an assertion not to be found in traditional Christian theology. There is, however, a sense in which it is most true to say that God is 'up there' or 'out there' and that is that 'God' is not simply another word for human life or experience at its most profound or intense. It is not clear, on this basic issue, which of the two uses the bishop has in mind.

This is a very significant area of confusion and it pinpoints what is a real situation of crisis in contemporary theology. This is 'the crisis of metaphor', and it bears on the discussions about 'myth' and symbolism to be found in a number of the extracts given in this series. Man as a finite being is bound to be a metaphor-making animal so long as he experiences intimations of realities outside or beyond what can be measured scientifically. This means, at the least, so long as he remains capable of aesthetic, moral, and mystical experience. The fact, for instance, that to indicate these experiences he uses the spatial language of a 'three-decker' universe ('up there', 'down there') is not the 'scandal' that Bultmann and Dr Robinson take it to be. This is a serious misplacing of what is the real 'stumbling-block' for twentieth-century man as far as Christian language is concerned. In fact the 'three-decker' universe is not a bad image to use in any talk about values and religious beliefs, at least for finite man in a space-time universe which is likely to be the condition of most of mankind in the foreseeable future. For spaceless man no doubt another image would be necessary, but until it is demonstrated that spacelessness is to be the permanent human state to try and dispense with spatial or temporal metaphor or even to be coy about its use is not a sign of maturity or progress. It indicates an inhuman and senseless attempt to try and jump out of our finite skin. The momentum of the human mind, as the poet Wallace Stevens put it, is towards abstraction. Part of the appeal of a 'demythologized' version of Christianity, suggested by Bultmann and others, and commended by Dr Robinson, is that it takes one away from the trying particularities of the concrete. But 'concretization', to use Bonhoeffer's term, is a necessary undertaking for the Christian religion as long as it is firmly rooted in an historical and particular Incarnation. It is this feature of the Christian religion which indicates where the real 'stumbling-block' for modern man has to be placed. This is precisely where St Paul put it, in the enigmatical ambiguity of a Christ who is so identified with the human scene as to be, seemingly, indistinguishable from it, except to the eyes of faith.

It would be generally true to say that all the theologians represented in this series took a view about the task of philosophy which has now become very unfashionable in Britain. They believed the job of the philosopher was to build up a world-view, a 'metaphysics'. Both Barth and Tillich shared this view. Barth suspected that the very 'world-view' inherent in philosophy would blur the distinctiveness of Christianity. Bultmann believed that 'existentialism' provided a coherent 'metaphysics' of human existence. Niebuhr and the earlier Bonhoeffer approached philosophy in the same way.

It is the special interest of Paul van Buren's *The Secular Meaning of the Gospel* (1963) that it discusses the relation between Christian theology and the type of linguistic or analytical philosophy which has developed in Britain and the United States. For philosophers like Ludwig Wittgenstein, G. E. Moore and A. J. Ayer the task of the philosopher is not to construct a 'world-view' but to analyse and classify language. The philosopher studies how language works and the meanings which we attach to statements. He seeks to establish ways of verifying the truth of the various assertions we make.

In the first wave of linguistic analysis popularized by A. J. Ayer's *Language, Truth and Logic* (1936) it was asserted that the only kind of language which had meaning was that which was scientifically verifiable. All other types of language, poetry, for example, or moral exhortation or religion, were said to be meaningless because they were not susceptible to this kind of verification. Philosophical linguistic analysis has modified this position in recent years, and the concern now is how to classify the uses of language and to discuss the types of meaning appropriate to each in relation to the contexts in which they are used.

Paul van Buren seeks to relate the exposition of Christian theology to this kind of linguistic philosophical analysis. Also he has in mind the wish expressed by Bonhoeffer that one ought to be seeking for a 'non-religious interpretation' of biblical and theological concepts. van Buren's book has been nicknamed 'The case of the disappearing gospel'. Certainly in the process of re-stating Christianity in 'non-religious' language he so dissolves traditional Christian theology that it is difficult to see what if anything a believer of former times would recognize in it as familiar.

In *The Secular Meaning of the Gospel* van Buren contended that there is a residual Christianity, even when one has abandoned the idea that any meaning can be attached to 'God' or the 'transcendent'. This remainder he turns into a kind of moral heroism. Christ becomes for all men a model, *the* paradigm, of 'openness' and freedom. The significance of Christ is that he has shown himself, and continues to show himself to be a potent example of these qualities.

The most recent phase of theology has been called the 'death of God' movement. This is the title of a book by Gabriel Vahanian, and it has been used to describe the work not only of Vahanian but of Thomas Altizer (*The Gospel of Christian Atheism*) and William Hamilton, *The Essence of Christianity*.

If one complained about confusion in *Honest to God* this complaint would have to be brought even more sharply against some of these theologians, especially Altizer, whose work is irritatingly rhapsodic just at the points where clarity of expression is most required. It is not at all easy to be sure of what exactly is being said. In one way Altizer seems to be saying that Nietzsche's cry, 'God is dead', still needs repeating, particularly since as far as modern man in a technological society is concerned belief in God as a transcendent reality upon whom mankind depends has no meaning, and is hopelessly irrelevant. Man must now look to his own resources as he prepares to take charge of his own evolution.

Another side of Altizer seems to be saying, again in a very

confused way, that Christians have been reluctant to come to realistic terms with the Incarnation, particularly with its corollary that Christ really died the death. This is a useful point because it is true that Christians have traditionally not only denied that Christ was born in the way that we are, but there remained for a long time in Christian theology, especially in the Greek church, the belief that Christ's human flesh was not mortal flesh as ours is.

Altizer wishes to press the reality of the *kenosis* or self-giving in Incarnation so that one can say with Charles Péguy, 'God too has faced death'. But Altizer seems to take *kenosis* to mean a literal self-annihilation. He speaks of the death of God as 'an historical event'. If these words mean anything Altizer is saying that in the Incarnation God, as it were, committed suicide. The death of God in Christ has freed us to become our own Christs, the result of the Incarnation being that God has diffused himself in the human race. This sounds like a new version of pantheism.

What is specially interesting in the 'death of God' theologians is the place which they are still willing to accord to Christ. In spite of form-criticism and the wave of scepticism which it produced both Altizer and Hamilton seem to believe that there is sufficient reliable information available about Jesus to warrant our thinking again about the ideal of the 'imitation of Christ'. This is interpreted along very different lines from Bonhoeffer's presentation of the *imitatio Christi*. It reminds one of what Kierkegaard called 'admiration of Christ', a heroic endeavour to reproduce his 'openness' and 'freedom' by sheer effort of will.

5

It is hazardous to suggest what is likely to be the prospect for theology in the rest of this century. However, it seems to me that four areas will provide material for special clarification: (1) There is first what I have called the 'crisis of metaphor' in modern theology. Theology and religious language stand or fall by metaphor and all that it implies about human life and human perception. The impulse to metaphor, to speak of one

• •

thing in terms of another, prompts the question whether the relation between appearance and reality may not be of the kind which religious belief suggests. The surrender of metaphor means the end of religion and, significantly, the death of what we have come to regard as distinctively human feelings. The French 'anti-novelist' Alain Robbe-Grillet is perfectly right to detect an important link between metaphor and religion. Robbe-Grillet wishes to get rid of metaphor because it implies some hidden relationship between man and the universe, and this takes us half-way to religion. Indeed, there is a 'crisis of metaphor' in modern literature as well as in modern theology. Bultmann can speak disparagingly of 'mere metaphors' and advocates 'demythologization' because myth, metaphor and symbol can be taken in a crude literal way, or can become obsolete. These are certainly hazards in the human situation, which often necessitate a drastic process of unlearning. But a worse fate, a greater hurt to the soul is to attempt to bring about a state of affairs where such hazards are no longer possible. It is damaging either to identify metaphor and actuality or to romanticize pantheistically (in a way that alarms Robbe-Grillet), but it is worse to believe that as individuals and as a generation we have gone beyond the need for metaphor. At stake, therefore, in the present 'crisis of metaphor' in literature and religion is nothing less than the humanization or dehumanization of man.

(2) There needs to be very much more exploration of what Tillich called 'correlation' between religion and the arts. Christians have lived too long with the assumption that while art may have aesthetic or pedagogical value, it is no serious avenue to truth. Art has been regarded as useful for those who cannot read, and need pictures, but not for the literate who having mastered discursive reasoning and the manipulation of abstractions have no need of the image. Art has therefore been taken by many theologians to be inferior to philosophy, and on the whole Christian theologians have preferred to cultivate relations with philosophers rather than artists. This is, however, to beg the question whether art is a way of knowing which is as truth-bearing, in its way, as philosophical or scientific method. Christians have surrendered with amazing ease to the notion that the image is a lesser form of truth than the con-

cept, as if image and concept were simply alternative ways of saying the same thing, except that the image helps those who have more imagination than logic. It is arguable that the Christian religion would have gained as much (perhaps more) from association with art as it has from philosophy, not only for general apologetic reasons, but for intellectual arguments with what Schleiermacher called its 'cultural despisers'.

(3) Thirdly, there is the continuing work of interpreting afresh the significance of Christ and in the immediate future this will have to include a thorough exploration of what it means to talk about the uniqueness of Christ and his finality.

In spite of the central place which it occupies in the structure of their beliefs, it has proved persistently difficult for Christians to take the Incarnation with full realism and to follow through its implications in a rigorously realistic way. It took Christians a very long time indeed to accept the belief that the Incarnation meant taking a human biology exactly like ours. What a struggle there was in the early Church to get accepted the belief that Christ really died the death in the way that we do! The history of the iconography of the crucifixion in art shows that it took nearly five centuries before a body of Christ appeared on the cross, and then it is very much a live Christ who, eyes open, stands on the cross as a royal warrior looking through the scene. It took the Christian Church nearly ten centuries before a really dead body of Christ appeared on the cross, and even then it was not a death in suffering and agony. It is another century and a half before a bleeding, suffering emaciated Christ with a crown of thorns appears in the representation of the crucifixion. This is a long time, but it has taken Christians even longer to come anywhere near accepting that the Incarnation involved taking a genuine human psychology of the kind that might mean that Christ had to find his way to religious belief in exactly the same way as everybody else, through faith, through acting on signs which, because they are ambiguous and our freedom is real, can always be 'stumbling-bocks' ('scandals' in the New Testament) that offend. Just as dangerous as a theology based on the 'God of the gaps' has been a 'Christology of the gaps', that is, a tendency to insert a capacity for full divine self-awareness on the part of the historical Jesus in some 'gap' in his psyche, or, so it has sometimes been suggested, in his subconscious!

The question of the finality of Christ suggests the fourth area in which it is likely that theology will be specially engaged in the immediate future: comparative religion, and especially comparative theology.

(4) In the contemporary world it sometimes appears that the 'ecumenical' movement of unbelief grows faster than that of belief, so that all religions are finding themselves on the same side of the fence as far as faith that human life has a transcendental significance is concerned. In this situation there needs to be more conversation between the theologies of the religions, particularly those whose history gives them a special kinship: Judaism, Christianity and Islam. If the Christian has to start thinking again about the meaning of Incarnation and the unique place which he assigns to Christ there is no more bracing company in which he could explore this question than that of the Jew and Muslim.

The present-day student of the Christian doctrines of the Trinity and the Incarnation might well begin with reflection on the familiar strictures on these doctrines that come from the Jew and the Muslim: that they violate the concept of the unity of God, and, by involving God in human history in a finite way, blaspheme against the majesty of God. The Christian will want to have as rich a doctrine that God is one as the Jew or the Muslim, and that God is known in historical event, and perhaps this is now more likely to be attained by going to school theologically with these two religions. Further the three religions of Judaism, Christianity and Islam have much to give each other in working out afresh for our own day the meaning of what it is to be human. Bishop Kenneth Cragg has shown how profound a realization of the nature of man comes from relating the Jewish/Christian concept of man made in the 'image of God' to the Muslim concept of man as God's 'caliph'.[1]

Much needs to be unlearned and relearned in this field. Judaism, Islam and Buddhism have suffered from misleading propagandist slogans in the past like 'Jewish legalism', 'Islam

[1] Kenneth Cragg, *The Privilege of Man*, London, 1968.

is the most materialistic and least religious of the religions',
'Buddhism is insensitive to suffering or social justice'. These
are Christian caricatures of the truth, and there is now a fresh
chance, especially in those western countries which are now
multi-religious, to rectify this distortion by mutual understanding in co-operative study.

BIOGRAPHICAL INTRODUCTION

Tillich has written his own autobiographical reflections in *The Protestant Era*, *The Interpretation of History* and in an essay at the beginning of *The Theology of Paul Tillich* (edited by Kegley and Bretall).

He was an exact contemporary of Karl Barth, being born in 1886 at Starzeddel in the German province of Brandenburg. Like Barth also, and indeed all the writers in this series, he came of clerical stock, his father being the village pastor. Tillich retained vivid memories of conversations with his father about philosophy and spoke of them in later life as 'the most happy instance of a positive relation to my father'. In common with Bultmann he had a country upbringing, but this seems to have made a much deeper impression on Tillich who speaks of his mystical feeling towards nature, the land and the soil. He had also the same feeling for the sea. He obviously reacted sensitively to his home life and says that the influence of life in a parish house with Lutheran school on one side and Gothic church on the other gave him his 'idea of the holy'. All this influenced profoundly the kind of theology which was to come later. He could see himself later as something of a nineteenth-century romantic with a deep sense of man's 'mystical' participation in nature and profound belief that man, finite and limited creature though he be, is able to experience the infinite.

In spite of his attachment to the country, he was greatly excited by his first visit to Berlin and says he felt 'extreme joy' when the family moved there in 1900. Tillich studied theology at the universities of Berlin, Tübingen and Halle, taking his doctorate in 1910 at Breslau. In 1912 he was ordained pastor and worked in the province of Brandenburg. During the 1914–18 war he served as an army chaplain. Important for his later development were his studies in art at this period, particularly early Christian mosaics. Tillich was to remain specially interested in religion and the arts and is the only thinker in the group represented in this series who attempted to construct a theology of culture.

In 1919 Tillich began his university teaching career in

Berlin, moving in 1924 to Marburg where he held the chair of theology. In 1925 he became professor of the philosophy of religion and social philosophy at Dresden. He also taught in Leipzig at this period. Then in 1929 he was appointed professor of philosophy at Frankfurt.

Tillich had become opposed to the Nazi movement long before 1933 when Hitler came to power. He was dismissed from his chair at Frankfurt. Reinhold Niebuhr happened to be in America that year, and arranged for Tillich to go to Union Theological Seminary, New York. He was appointed professor of philosophical theology. This was the beginning of Tillich's American period which proved to be specially happy and fruitful. He spoke warmly of what he owed to Union, especially its community life after the 'extreme individualism of one's academic existence in Germany'. Here also he developed his interests in religious socialism which went back to his student days.

After his retirement in 1955 he was invited to become professor at Harvard University. He taught also in the University of Chicago. Tillich died on 27 October 1965.

SELECTIONS

1 THEOLOGY AND THEOLOGICAL METHOD

(a) *The Method of Correlation*

[Tillich suggests that the 'method of correlation' best expresses the relation between theology and philosophy. Unlike Barth, Tillich believed that theology can only be done in close association with philosophy. For him man is such a kind of being that a full analysis of himself would raise questions about the relation between finite and infinite, time and eternity, etc. Such an analysis is the task of philosophy, especially existentialist philosophy. It is to these basic questions raised by such a philosophical analysis that theology addresses itself.]

This method tries to overcome the conflict between the naturalistic and supernaturalistic methods which imperils not only any real progress in the work of systematic theology but also any possible effect of theology on the secular world. The method of correlation shows, at every point of Christian thought, the interdependence between the ultimate questions to which philosophy (as well as pre-philosophical thinking) is driven and the answers given in the Christian message.

Philosophy cannot answer ultimate or existential questions *qua* philosophy. If the philosopher tries to answer them (and all creative philosophers have tried to do so), he becomes a theologian. And, conversely, theology cannot answer those questions without accepting their presuppositions and implications. Question and answer determine each other; if they are separated, the traditional answers become unintelligible, and the actual questions remain unanswered. The method of correlation aims to overcome this situation. In the chapter on 'Philosophy and Theology' (as well as in all my work in systematic theology) the method is explained and applied. Such a method is truly dialectical and therefore opposed to the supernaturalism of later Barthianism as well as to any other type of orthodoxy and fundamentalism. Philosophy and theology are not separated, and they are not identical, but they are correlated, and their correlation is the methodological problem of a Protestant theology . . .

(FROM: *The Protestant Principle*, p. xlii.)

. . . Theology formulates the questions implied in human existence, and theology formulates the answers implied in divine self-manifestation under the guidance of the questions implied in human existence. This is a circle which drives man to a point where question and answer are not separated. This point, however, is not a moment in time. It belongs to man's essential being, to the unity of his finitude with the infinity in which he was created and from which he is separated. A symptom of both the essential unity and the existential separation of finite man from his infinity is his ability to ask about the infinite to which he belongs: the fact that he must ask about it indicates that he is separated from it.

The answers implied in the event of revelation are meaningful only in so far as they are in correlation with questions concerning the whole of our existence, with existential questions. Only those who have experienced the shock of transitoriness, the anxiety in which they are aware of their finitude, the threat of non-being, can understand what the notion of God means. Only those who have experienced the tragic ambiguities of our historical existence and have totally questioned the meaning of existence can understand what the symbol of the Kingdom of God means. Revelation answers questions which have been asked and always will be asked because they are 'we ourselves'. Man is the question he asks about himself, before any qustion has been formulated. It is, therefore, not surprising that the basic questions were formulated very early in the history of mankind. Every analysis of the mythological material shows this.[1] Nor is it surprising that the same questions appear in early childhood as every observation of children shows. Being human means asking the question of one's own being and living under the impact of the answers given to this question. And, conversely, being human means

[1] Cf. H. Gunkel, *The Legends of Genesis* (Chicago: Open Court Pub. Co., 1901).

receiving answers to the question of one's own being and asking questions under the impact of the answers.

In using the method of correlation, systematic theology proceeds in the following way: it makes an analysis of the human situation out of which the existential questions arise. and it demonstrates that the symbols used in the Christian message are the answers to these questions. The analysis of the human situation is done in terms which today are called 'existential'. Such analyses are much older than existentialism; they are, indeed, as old as man's thinking about himself, and they have been expressed in various kinds of conceptualization since the beginning of philosophy. Whenever man has looked at his world he has found himself in it as a part of it. But he also has realized that he is a stranger in the world of objects, unable to penetrate it beyond a certain level of scientific analysis. And then he has become aware of the fact that he himself is the door to the deeper levels of reality, that in his own existence he has the only possible approach to existence itself.[1] This does not mean that man is more approachable than other objects as material for scientific research. The opposite is the case! It does mean that the immediate experience of one's own existing reveals something of the nature of existence generally. Whoever has penetrated into the nature of his own finitude can find the traces of finitude in everything that exists. And he can ask the question implied in his finitude as the question implied in finitude universally. In doing so he does not formulate a doctrine of man; he expresses a doctrine of existence as experienced in him as man. When Calvin in the opening sentences of the *Institutes* correlates our knowledge of God with our knowledge of man, he does not speak of the doctrine of man as such and of the doctrine of God as such. He speaks of man's misery, which gives the existential basis for his understanding of God's glory, and of God's glory, which gives the essential basis for man's understanding of his

---

[1] Cf. Augustine's doctrine of truth dwelling in the soul and transcending it at the same time; the mystical identification of the ground of being with the ground of self; the use of psychological categories for ontological purposes in Paracelsus, Böhme, Schelling, and in the 'philosophy of life' from Schopenhauer to Bergson; Heidegger's notion of 'Dasein' (being there) as the form of human existence and the entrance to ontology.

misery. Man as existing, representing existence generally and
asking the question implied in his existence, is one side of the
cognitive correlation to which Calvin points, the other side
being the divine majesty. In the initial sentences of his
theological system Calvin expresses the essence of the method
of correlation.[1]

The analysis of the human situation employs materials made
available by man's creative self-interpretation in all realms
of culture. Philosophy contributes, but so do poetry, drama,
the novel, therapeutic psychology, and sociology. The theologian organizes these materials in relation to the answer given
by the Christian message. In the light of this message he may
make an analysis of existence which is more penetrating than
that of most philosophers. Nevertheless, it remains a philosophical analysis. The analysis of existence, including the
development of the questions implicit in existence, is a philosophical task, even if it is performed by a theologian, and even
if the theologian is a reformer like Calvin. The difference
between the philosopher who is not a theologian and the
theologian who works as a philosopher in analysing human
existence is only that the former tries to give an analysis
which will be part of a broader philosophical work while the
latter tries to correlate the material of his analysis with the
theological concepts he derives from the Christian faith. This
does not make the philosophical work of the theologian
heteronomous. As a theologian he does not tell himself what
is philosophically true. As a philosopher he does not tell
himself what is theologically true. But he cannot help seeing
human existence and existence generally in such a way that
the Christian symbols appear meaningful and understandable
to him. His eyes are partially focused by his ultimate concern,
which is true of every philosopher. Nevertheless, his act of
seeing is autonomous, for it is determined only by the object
as it is given in his experience. If he sees something he did
not expect to see in the light of his theological answer, he

---

[1] 'The knowledge of ourselves is not only an incitement to seek after
God, but likewise a considerable assistance towards finding him. On
the other hand, it is plain that no man can arrive at the true knowledge
of himself, without having first contemplated the divine character, and
then descended to the consideration of his own' (John Calvin,
Institutes, I, 48).

holds fast to what he has seen and reformulates the theological answer. He is certain that nothing he sees can change the substance of his answer, because this substance is the *logos* of being, manifest in Jesus as the Christ. If this were not his presupposition, he would have to sacrifice either his philosophical honesty or his theological concern.

The Christian message provides the answers to the questions implied in human existence. These answers are contained in the revelatory events on which Christianity is based and are taken by systematic theology *from* the sources, *through* the medium, *under* the norm. Their content cannot be derived from the questions, that is, from an analysis of human existence. They are 'spoken' *to* human existence from beyond it. Otherwise they would not be answers, for the question is human existence itself. But the relation is more involved than this, since it is correlation. There is a mutual dependence between question and answer. In respect to content the Christian answers are dependent on the revelatory events in which they appear; in respect to form they are dependent on the structure of the questions which they answer. God is the answer to the question implied in human finitude. This answer cannot be derived from the analysis of existence. However, if the notion of God appears in systematic theology in correlation with the threat of non-being which is implied in existence, God must be called the infinite power of being which resists the threat of non-being. In classical theology this is being-itself. If anxiety is defined as the awareness of being finite, God must be called the infinite ground of courage. In classical theology this is universal providence. If the notion of the Kingdom of God appears in correlation with the riddle of our historical existence, it must be called the meaning, fulfilment, and unity of history. In this way an interpretation of the traditional symbols of Christianity is achieved which preserves the power of these symbols and which opens them to the questions elaborated by our present analysis of human existence.

(FROM: *Systematic Theology*, I, pp. 69–72.)

. . . The term 'philosophical theology' points to a theology that has a philosophical character. What does this mean?

First of all, it implies that there is a theology that has *not* a philosophical but some other character. This, indeed, is the case. As long as theological thought has existed, there have been two types of theology, a philosophical one and—let me call it—a 'kerygmatic' one. Kerygmatic is derived from the New Testament word *kerygma*, 'message'. It is a theology that tries to reproduce the content of the Christian message in an ordered and systematic way, without referring to philosophy. In contrast to it, philosophical, theology, although based on the same *kerygma*, tries to explain the contents of the *kerygma*, in close interrelation with philosophy. The tension and mutual fertilization between these two types is a main event and a fortunate one in all history of Christian thought. The fight of the traditionalists of the early church against the rising logos-Christology, the struggle between the mystics and dialecticians in the early Middle Ages, between Biblicism and scholasticism in the later Middle Ages, between the Reformers and the Aristotelian scholastics, the attack of the Ritschlians on speculative theology, and of the Barthians on a philosophy of religion—all this and much more was the consequence of the existence of a philosophical and a kerygmatic theology. The duality is natural. It is implied in the very word 'theology', the syllable 'theo' pointing to the *kerygma*, in which God is revealed, and the syllable 'logy' pointing to the endeavour of human reason to receive the message. This implies further that kerygmatic and philosophical theology demand each other and are wrong in the moment in which they become exclusive. No kerygmatic theology ever existed which did not use philosophical terms and methods. And no philosophical theology ever existed—deserving the name 'theology' —which did not try to explain the content of the message. Therefore, the theological ideal is the complete unity of both types, an ideal which is reached only by the greatest theologians and even by them only approximately. The fact that every human creativity has its typological limitations makes it desirable that theological faculties should include a representative of kerygmatic and one of philosophical theology, whether the latter is called apologetics, speculative theology, Christian philosophy of religion, or philosophical theology. The church cannot do without this type, just as, of course, it cannot dispense with the kerygmatic type.

(FROM: *The Protestant Principle*, pp. 93–4.)

(b) Faith and Doubt in the Theologian

[In this passage Tillich touches on the question of the relationship of theology to religion, and in particular the matter of the theologian's own faith. The 'philosopher of religion' is more detached from his subject than the 'theologian', argues Tillich, since the latter, as one who participates in the particular beliefs of a specific religious community, stands inside 'the theological circle'. But the theologian also needs to be 'distanced' from religion, to know what it is like to be outside this circle.]

But the circle within which the theologian works is narrower than that of the philosopher of religion. He adds to the 'mystical *a priori*' the criterion of the Christian message. While the philosopher of religion tries to remain general and abstract in his concepts, as the concept 'religion' itself indicates, the theologian is consciously and by intention specific and concrete. The difference, of course, is not absolute. Since the experiential basis of every philosophy of religion is partly determined by the cultural tradition to which it belongs—even mysticism is culturally conditioned—it inescapably includes concrete and special elements. The philosopher as philosopher, however, tries to abstract from these elements and to create generally valid concepts concerning religion. The theologian, on the other hand, claims the universal validity of the Christian message in spite of its concrete and special character. He does not justify this claim by abstracting from the concreteness of the message but by stressing its unrepeatable uniqueness. He enters the theological circle with a concrete commitment. He enters it as a member of the Christian Church to perform one of the essential functions of the Church—its theological self-interpretation.

The 'scientific' theologian wants to be more than a philosopher of religion. He wants to interpret the Christian message generally with the help of his method. This puts before him two alternatives. He may subsume the Christian message under his concept of religion. Then Christianity is considered to be one example of religious life beside other examples, certainly the highest religion, but not the final one and not unique. Such a theology does not enter the theological circle. It keeps itself within the religious-philosophical circle and its indefinite horizons—horizons which beckon towards a future which is open for new and perhaps higher examples of religion. The scientific theologian, in spite of his desire to be a theologian, remains a philosopher of religion. Or he becomes really a theologian, an interpreter of his Church and its claim to uniqueness and universal validity. Then he enters the theological circle and should admit that he has done so and stop speaking of himself as a scientific theologian in the ordinary sense of 'scientific'.

But even the man who has entered the theological circle consciously and openly faces another serious problem. Being inside the circle, he must have made an existential decision; he must be in the situation of faith. But no one can say of himself that he is in the situation of faith. No one can call himself a theologian, even if he is called to be a teacher of theology. Every theologian is committed *and* alienated; he is always in faith *and* in doubt; he is inside *and* outside the theological circle. Sometimes the one side prevails, sometimes the other; and he is never certain which side really prevails. Therefore, one criterion alone can be applied: a person can be a theologian as long as he acknowledges the content of the theological circle as his ultimate concern. Whether this is true does not depend on his intellectual or moral or emotional state; it does not depend on the intensity and certitude of faith; it does not depend on the power of regeneration or the grade of sanctification. Rather it depends on his being ultimately concerned with the Christian message even if he is sometimes inclined to attack and to reject it.

(FROM: *Systematic Theology*, I, pp. 12–13.)

(c) *Paradox, logic and symbols in religious language*

[In these two passages Tillich deals first with the difficult question of the relation between the language of paradox and the language of logic. Paradoxical language, as a matter of words, looks logically self-contradictory, but it makes sense, Tillich implies, in experience. Paradoxical language is used, not to defy the rules of logic, but to indicate a reality which, while it goes beyond human rationality, does not contradict it.

In the second extract Tillich turns to the meaning and use of symbols, whether in words or in art. One of the gains of modern linguistic philosophy has been to show that there is a wide variety in the uses of language: scientific, poetic, moral etc. Scientific language prefers to use words which mean one thing at a time whereas poetic language depends upon words meaning several things simultaneously.

Tillich distinguishes 'symbols' from 'signs'. Signs indicate what they stand for in a conventional way and have a limited suggestiveness. New signs are easily invented and being conventional may be changed without difficulty. For instance red as a traffic sign for 'stop' could be changed to purple. Symbols are much more potent. They open up new levels of meaning and enhance human powers of perception. They are irreplaceable. This has an important bearing on the 'demythologizing' controversy (see Vol. 2, pp. 64 ff). Symbols, says Tillich, participate in the reality to which they point. By this he seems to mean that when one is truly reacting to an effective symbol one has the experience of responding at the same time to another reality. This makes it inevitable, especially perhaps in religion, that people will identify the symbol with this reality. That however would be to turn the symbol into an idol.]

. . . Theological dialectics does not violate the principle of logical rationality. The same is true of paradoxical statements in religion and theology. When Paul points to his situation as an apostle and to that of Christians generally in a series of *paradoxa* (2 Corinthians), he does not intend to say something illogical; he intends to give the adequate, understandable, and therefore logical expression of the infinite tensions of Christian existence. When he speaks about the paradox of the justification of the sinner (in Luther's formula, *simul peccator et iustus*),[1] and when John speaks about the Logos becoming flesh (later expressed in the *paradoxa* of the creed of Chalcedon),[2] neither of them wishes to indulge in logical contradictions.[3] They want to express the conviction that God's acting transcends all possible human expectations and all necessary human preparations. It transcends, but it does not destroy, finite reason; for God acts through the Logos which is the transcendent and transcending source of the *logos* structure of thought and being. God does not annihilate the expressions of his own Logos. The term 'paradox' should be defined carefully, and paradoxical language should be used with discrimination. Paradoxical means 'against the opinion', namely, the opinion of finite reason. Paradox points to the fact that in God's acting finite reason is superseded but not annihilated; it expresses this fact in terms which are not logically contradictory but which are supposed to point beyond the realm in which finite reason is applicable. This is indicated by the ecstatic state in which all biblical and classical theological *paradoxa* appear. The confusion begins when these *paradoxa* are brought down to the level of genuine logical contradictions and people are asked to sacrifice reason in order to accept senseless combinations of words as divine wisdom. But Christianity does not demand such intellectual 'good words' from anyone, just as it does not ask artificial 'works' of practical asceticism. There is, in the last analysis, only *one* genuine paradox in the Christian message—the appearance of that which conquers existence under the conditions of existence. Incarnation, redemption, justification, etc., are implied in this paradoxical event. It is not a logical contradiction which makes it a paradox but the fact that it transcends all human expectations and possibilities. It breaks into the context of experience or reality, but it cannot be derived from it. The acceptance of this paradox is not the acceptance of the absurd, but it is the state of being grasped by the power of that which breaks into our experience

---

[1] 'Sinner and righteous at one and the same time' (Ed.).

[2] Council of Chalcedon A.D. 451. The definition of this Council spoke of Christ paradoxically as 'truly God and truly man' (Ed.).

[3] It is the mistake of Brunner in *The Mediator* that he makes the offence of logical rationality the criterion of Christian truth. This 'offence' is neither that of Kierkegaard nor that of the New Testament.

from above it. Paradox in religion and theology does not conflict with the principle of logical rationality. Paradox has its logical place . . .

(FROM : *Systematic Theology*, I, pp. 63-4.)

. . . The fact that there is so much discussion about the meaning of symbols going on in this country as well as in Europe is a symptom of something deeper, something both negative and positive in its import. It is a symptom of the fact that we are in a confusion of language in theology and philosophy and related subjects which has hardly been surpassed at any time in history. Words do not communicate to us any more what they originally did and what they were invented to communicate. This has something to do with the fact that our present culture has no clearing house such as medieval scholasticism was, Protestant scholasticism in the seventeenth century at least tried to be, and philosophers like Kant tried to renew. We have no such clearing house, and this is the one point at which we might be in sympathy with the present day so-called logical positivists or symbolic logicians or logicians generally. They at least try to produce a clearing house. The only criticism is that this clearing house is a very small room, perhaps only a corner of a house, and not a real house. It excludes most of life. But it could become useful if it increased in reach and acceptance of realities beyond the mere logical calculus.

The positive point is that we are in a process in which a very important thing is being rediscovered: namely, that there are levels of reality of great difference, and that these different levels demand different approaches and different languages; not everything in reality can be grasped by the language which is most adequate for mathematical sciences. The insight into this situation is the most positive side of the fact that the problem of symbols is again taken seriously.

Let us proceed with the intention of clearing concepts as much as we are able, and let us take five steps, the first of which is the discussion of 'symbols and signs'. Symbols are similar to signs in one decisive respect: both symbols and signs point beyond themselves to something else. The typical sign, for instance the red light at the corner of the street, does not point to itself but it points to the necessity of cars stopping. And every symbol points beyond itself to a reality for which it stands. In this, symbols and signs have an essential identity—they point beyond themselves. And this is the reason that the confusion of language mentioned above has also conquered the discussion about symbols for centuries and has produced confusion between signs and symbols. The first step in any clearing up of the meaning of symbols is to distinguish it from the meaning of signs.

The difference, which is a fundamental difference between them, is that signs do not participate in any way in the reality and power of that to which they point. Symbols, although they are not the same as that which they symbolize, participate in its meaning and power. The difference between symbol and sign is the participation in the symbolized reality which characterizes the symbols, and the non-participation in the 'pointed-to' reality which characterizes a sign. For example, letters of the alphabet as they are written, an 'A' or an 'R' do not participate in the sound to which they point; on the other hand, the flag participates in the power of the king or the nation for which it stands and which it symbolizes. There has, therefore, been a fight since the days of William Tell as to how to behave in the presence of the flag. This would be meaningless if the flag did not participate as a symbol in the power of that which it symbolizes. The whole monarchic idea is itself entirely incomprehensible, if you do not understand that the king always is both: on the one hand, a symbol of the power of the group of which he is the king and on the other hand, he who exercises partly (never fully, of course) this power.

But something has happened which is very dangerous for all our attempts to find a clearing house for the concepts of symbols and signs. The mathematician has usurped the term 'symbol' for mathematical 'sign', and this makes a disentaglement of the confusion almost impossible. The only thing we can do is to distinguish different groups, signs which are called symbols, and genuine symbols. The mathematical signs are signs which are wrongly called symbols.

Language is a very good example of the difference between

signs and symbols. Words in a language are signs for a meaning which they express. The word 'desk' is a sign which
points to something quite different—namely, the thing on
which a paper is lying and at which we might be looking.
This has nothing to do with the word 'desk', with these four
letters. But there are words in every language which are more
than this, and in the moment in which they get connotations
which go beyond something to which they point as signs,
then they can become symbols; and this is a very important
distinction for any speaker. He can speak almost completely
in signs, reducing the meaning of his words almost to mathematical signs, and this is the absolute ideal of the logical
positivist. The other pole of this is liturgical or poetic language
where words have a power through centuries, or more than
centuries. They have connotations in situations in which they
appear so that they cannot be replaced. They have become
not only signs pointing to a meaning which is defined, but
also symbols standing for a reality in the power of which they
participate.

Now we come to a second consideration dealing with the
functions of symbols. The first function is implied in what
has already been said—namely, the representative function.
The symbol represents something which is not itself, for which
it stands and in the power and meaning of which it participates.
This is a basic function of every symbol, and therefore, if
that word had not been used in so many other ways, one
could perhaps even translate 'symbolic' as 'representative',
but for some reason that is not possible. If the symbols stand
for something which they are not, then the question is, 'Why
do we not have that for which they stand directly? Why do
we need symbols at all?' And now we come to something
which is perhaps the main function of the symbol—namely,
the opening up of levels of reality which otherwise are hidden
and cannot be grasped in any other way.

Every symbol opens up a level of reality for which non-
symbolic speaking is inadequate. Let us interpret this, or
explain this, in terms of artistic symbols. The more we try
to enter into the meaning of symbols, the more we become
aware that it is a function of art to open up levels of reality;

in poetry, in visual art, and in music, levels of reality are
opened up which can be opened up in no other way. Now if
this is the function of art then certainly artistic creations have
symbolic character. You can take that which a landscape of
Rubens, for instance, mediates to you. You cannot have this
experience in any other way than through this painting made
by Rubens. This landscape has some heroic character; it has
character of balance, of colours, of weights, of values, and so
on. All this is very external. What this mediates to you cannot
be expressed in any other way than through the painting itself.
The same is true also in the relationship of poetry and philosophy. The temptation may often be to confuse the issue by
bringing too many philosophical concepts into a poem. Now
this is really the problem; one cannot do this. If one uses
philosophical language or scientific language, it does not
mediate the same thing which is mediated in the use of really
poetic language without a mixture of any other language.

This example may show what is meant by the phrase 'opening up of levels of reality'. But in order to do this, something
else must be opened up—namely, levels of the soul, levels of
our interior reality. And they must correspond to the levels
in exterior reality which are opened up by a symbol. So every
symbol is two-edged. It opens up reality and it opens up the
soul. There are, of course, people who are not opened up by
music or who are not opened up by poetry, or more of them
(especially in Protestant America) who are not opened up
at all by visual arts. The 'opening up' is a two-sided function—
namely, reality in deeper levels and the human soul in special
levels.

If this is the function of symbols then it is obvious that
symbols cannot be replaced by other symbols. Every symbol
has a special function which is just *it* and cannot be replaced
by more or less adequate symbols. This is different from signs,
for signs can always be replaced. If one finds that a green
light is not so expedient as perhaps a blue light (this is not
true, but could be true), then we simply put on a blue light,
and nothing is changed. But a symbolic word (such as the
word 'God') cannot be replaced. No symbol can be replaced
when used in its special function. So one asks rightly, 'How

do symbols arise, and how do they come to an end?' As different from signs, symbols are born and die. Signs are consciously invented and removed. This is a fundamental difference.

'Out of what womb are symbols born?' Out of the womb which is usually called today the 'group unconscious' or 'collective unconscious', or whatever you want to call it— out of a group which acknowledges, in this thing, this word, this flag, or whatever it may be, its own being. It is not invented intentionally; and even if somebody would try to invent a symbol, as sometimes happens, then it becomes a symbol only if the unconscious of a group says 'yes' to it. It means that something is opened up by it in the sense which I have just described. Now this implies further that in the moment in which this inner situation of the human group to a symbol has ceased to exist, then the symbol dies. The symbol does not 'say' anything any more. In this way, all of the polytheistic gods have died; the situation in which they were born, has changed or does not exist any more, and so the symbols died. But there are events which cannot be described in terms of intention and invention.

Now we come to a third consideration—namely, the nature of religious symbols. Religious symbols do exactly the same thing as all symbols do—namely, they open up a level of reality, which otherwise is not opened at all, which is hidden. We can call this the depth dimension of reality itself, the dimension of reality which is the ground of every other dimension and every other depth, and which therefore, is not one level beside the others but is the fundamental level, the level below all other levels, the level of being itself, or the ultimate power of being. Religious symbols open up the experience of the dimension of this depth in the human soul. If a religious symbol has ceased to have this function, then it dies. And if new symbols are born, they are born out of a changed relationship to the ultimate ground of being, i.e., to the Holy.

The dimension of ultimate reality is the dimension of the Holy. And so we can also say, religious symbols are symbols of the Holy. As such they participate in the holiness of the

Holy according to our basic definition of a symbol. But participation is not identity; they are not themselves *the* Holy. The wholly transcendent transcends every symbol of the Holy. Religious symbols are taken from the infinity of material which the experienced reality gives us. Everything in time and space has become at some time in the history of religion a symbol for the Holy. And this is naturally so, because everything that is in the world we encounter rests on the ultimate ground of being. This is the key to the otherwise extremely confusing history of religion. Those of you who have looked into this seeming chaos of the history of religion in all periods of history from the earliest primitive to the latest developments, will be extremely confused about the chaotic character of this development. They key which makes order out of this chaos is comparatively simple. It is that everything in reality can impress itself as a symbol for a special relationship of the human mind to its own ultimate ground and meaning. So in order to open up the seemingly closed door to this chaos of religious symbols, one simply has to ask, 'What is the relationship to the ultimate which is symbolized in these symbols?' And then they cease to be meaningless; and they become, on the contrary, the most revealing creations of the human mind, the most genuine ones, the most powerful ones, those who control the human consciousness, and perhaps even more the unconsciousness, and have therefore this tremendous tenacity which is characteristic of all religious symbols in the history of religion.

Religion, as everything in life, stands under the law of ambiguity, 'ambiguity' meaning that it is creative and destructive at the same time. Religion has its holiness and its unholiness, and the reason for this is obvious from what has been said about religious symbolism. Religious symbols point symbolically to that which transcends all of them. But since, as symbols, they participate in that to which they point, they always have the tendency (in the human mind, of course) to replace that to which they are supposed to point, and to become ultimate in themselves. And in the moment in which they do this, they become idols. All idolatry is nothing else than the absolutizing of symbols of the Holy, and making them identical with the Holy itself. In this way, for instance, holy persons can become a god. Ritual acts can take on unconditional validity, although they are only expressions of a special situation. In all sacramental activities of religion, in all holy objects, holy books, holy doctrines, holy rites, you find this danger which we will call 'demonization'. They become demonic at the moment in which they become elevated to the unconditional and ultimate character of the Holy itself.

Now we turn to a fourth consideration—namely, the levels of religious symbols. There are two fundamental levels in all religious symbols: the transcendent level, the level which goes *beyond* the empirical reality we encounter, and the immanent level, the level which we find *within* the encounter with reality. Let us look at the first level, the transcendent level. The basic symbol on the transcendent level would be God himself. But we cannot simply say that God is a symbol. We must always say two things about him: we must say that there is a non-symbolic element in our image of God—namely, that he is ultimate reality, being itself, ground of being, power of being; and the other, that he is the highest being in which everything that we have does exist in the most perfect way. If we say this we have in our mind the image of a highest being, a being with the characteristics of highest perfection. That means we have a symbol for that which is not symbolic in the idea of God—namely, 'Being Itself'.

It is important to distinguish these two elements in the idea of God. Thus all of these discussions going on about God being a person or not a person, God being similar to other beings or not similar, these discussions which have a great impact on the destruction of the religious experience through false interpretations of it, could be overcome if we would say, 'Certainly the awareness of something unconditional is in itself what it is, is not symbolic'. We can call it *'Being Itself'*, *esse qua esse, esse ipsum*, as the scholastics did. But in our relationship to this ultimate we symbolize and must symbolize. We could not be in communication with God if he were only 'ultimate being'. But in our relationship to him we encounter him with the highest of what we ourselves are, *person*. And so in the symbolic form of speaking about him, we have both that which transcends infinitely our experience of ourselves as persons, and that which is so adequate to our being persons that we can say, 'Thou' to God, and can pray to him. And these two elements must be preserved. If we preserve only the element of the unconditional, then no relationship to God is possible. If we preserve only the element of the ego-thou relationship, as it is called today, we lose the element of the divine—namely, the unconditional which transcends subject and object and all other polarities. This is the first point on the transcendent level.

The second is the qualities, the attributes of God, whatever you say about him: that he is love, that he is mercy, that he is power, that he is omniscient, that he is omnipresent, that he is almighty. These attributes of God are taken from experienced qualities we have ourselves. They cannot be applied to God in the literal sense. If this is done, it leads to an infinite amount of absurdities. This again is one of the reasons for the destruction of religion through wrong communicative interpretation of it. And again the symbolic character of these qualities must be maintained consistently. Otherwise, every speaking about the divine becomes absurd.

A third element on the transcendent level is the acts of God, for example, when we say, 'He has created the world', 'He has sent his son', 'He will fulfill the world'. In all these temporal, causal, and other expressions we speak symbolically of God. As an example, look at the one small sentence: '*God has sent his son.*' Here we have in the word 'has' temporality. But God is beyond *our* temporality, though not beyond every temporality. Here is space; 'sending somebody' means moving him from one place to another place. This certainly is speaking symbolically, although spatiality is in God as an element in his creative ground. We say that he 'has sent'—that means that he has caused something. In this way God is subject to the category of causality. And when we speak of him and his Son, we have two different substances and apply the category of substance to him. Now all this, if taken literally, is absurd. If it is taken symbolically, it is a profound expression, the ultimate Christian expression, of the relationship between God and man in the Christian experience. But to distinguish these two kinds of speech, the non-symbolic and the symbolic, in such a point is so important that if we are not able to make understandable to our contemporaries that we speak symbolically when we use such language, they will rightly turn away from us, as from people who still live in absurdities and superstitions.

Now consider the immanent level, the level of the appearances of the divine in time and space. Here we have first of all the incarnations of the divine, different beings in time and space, divine beings transmuted into animals or men or any kinds of other beings as they appear in time and space. This is often forgotten by those within Christianity who like to use in every second theological proposition the word 'incarnation'. They forget that this is not an especially Christian characteristic, because incarnation is something which happens in paganism all the time. The divine beings always incarnate in different forms. That is very easy in paganism. This is not the real distinction between Christianity and other religions.

Here we must say something about the relationships of the transcendent to the immanent level just in connection with the incarnation idea. Historically, one must say that preceding both of them was the situation in which the transcendent and immanent were not distinguished. In the Indonesian doctrine of 'Mana', that divine mystical power which permeates all reality, we have some divine presence which is both immanent in everything as a hidden power, and at the same time transcendent, something which can be grasped only through very difficult ritual activities known to the priest.

Out of this identity of the immanent and the transcendent, the gods of the great mythologies have developed in Greece and in the Semitic nations and in India. There we find incarnations as the immanent element of the divine. The more transcendent the gods become, the more incarnations of personal or sacramental character are needed in order to overcome the remoteness of the divine which develops with the strengthening of the transcendent element.

And from this follows the second element in the immanent religious symbolism, namely, the sacramental. The sacramental is nothing else than some reality becoming the bearer of the Holy in a special way and under special circumstances. In this sense, the Lord's Supper, or better the materials in the Lord's Supper, are symbolic. Now you will ask perhaps, 'only symbolic?' That sounds as if there were something more than symbolic, namely, 'literal'. But the literal is not more but less than symbolic. If we speak of those dimensions of reality which we cannot approach in any other way than by symbols, then symbols are not used in terms of 'only' but in terms of that which is necessary, of that which we *must* apply. Sometimes, because of nothing more than the confusion of signs with symbols, the phrase 'only a symbol' means 'only a sign'. And then the question is justified. 'Only a sign?' 'No.' The sacrament is not only a sign. In the famous discussion between Luther and Zwingli, in Marburg in 1529, it was just this point on which the discussion was held. Luther wanted to maintain the genuinely symbolic character of the elements, but Zwingli said that the sacramental materials, bread and wine, are 'only symbolic'. Thus Zwingli meant that they are only signs pointing to a story of the past. Even in that period there was semantic confusion. And let us not be misled by this. In the real sense of symbol, the sacramental materials are symbols. But if the symbol is used as *only* symbol (i.e., only signs), then of course the sacramental materials are more than this.

Then there is the third element on the immanent level. Many things—like special parts of the church building, like the candles, like the water at the entrance of the Roman Church, like the cross in all churches, especially Protestant churches—were originally only signs, but in use became symbols; call them sign-symbols, signs which have become symbols.

And now a last consideration—namely, the truth of religious symbols. Here we must distinguish a negative, a positive, and an absolute statement. First the negative statement. Symbols are independent of any empirical criticism. You cannot kill a symbol by criticism in terms of natural sciences or in terms of historical research. As was said, symbols can only die if the situation in which they have been created has passed. They are not on a level on which empirical criticism can dismiss them. Here are two examples, both connected with Mary, the mother of Jesus, as Holy Virgin. First of all you have here a symbol which has died in Protestantism by the changed situation of the relation to God. The special, direct, immediate relationship to God, makes any mediating power impossible. Another reason which has made this symbol disappear is the negation of the ascetic element which is implied in the glorification of virginity. And as long as the Protestant religious situation lasts it cannot be re-established. It has not died because Protestant scholars have said, 'Now there is no empirical reason for saying all this about the Holy Virgin'. There certainly is not, but this the Roman Church also knows. But the Roman Church sticks to it on the basis of its tremendous symbolic power which step by step brings her nearer to Trinity itself, especially in the development of the last decade. If this should ever be completed as is now discussed in groups of the Roman Church, Mary would become co-Saviour with Jesus. Then, whether this is admitted or not, she is actually taken into the divinity itself.

Another example is the story of the virginal birth of Jesus. This is from the point of view of historical research a most obviously legendary story, unknown to Paul and to John. It is a late creation, trying to make understandable the full possession of the divine Spirit of Jesus of Nazareth. But again its legendary character is not the reason why this symbol will die or has died in many groups of people, in even quite conservative groups within the Protestant churches. The reason is different. The reason is that it is theologically quasi-heretical. It takes away one of the fundamental doctrines of Chalcedon, viz., the classical Christian doctrine that the full humanity of Jesus must be maintained beside his whole divinity. A human being who has no human father has no full humanity. This story then has to be criticized on inner-symbolic grounds, but not on historical grounds. This is the negative statement about the truth of religious symbols. Their truth is their adequacy to the religious situation in which they are created, and their inadequacy to another situation is their untruth. In the last sentence both the positive and the negative statement about symbols are contained.

Religion is ambiguous and every religious symbol may become idolatrous, may be demonized, may elevate itself to ultimate validity although nothing is ultimate but the ultimate itself; no religious doctrine and no religious ritual may be. If Christianity claims to have a truth superior to any other truth in its symbolism, then it is the symbol of the cross in which this is expressed, the cross of the Christ. He who himself embodies the fullness of the divine's presence sacrifices himself in order not to become an idol, another god beside God, a god into whom the disciples wanted to make him. And therefore the decisive story is the story in which he accepts the title 'Christ' when Peter offers it to him. He accepts it under the one condition that he has to go to Jerusalem to suffer and to die, which means to deny the idolatrous tendency even with respect to himself. This is at the same time the criterion of all other symbols, and it is the criterion to which every Christian church should subject itself.

[FROM: *Theology of Culture*, pp. 53–67.]

(d) The Bible as a Source for Christian Theology

[It is instructive to compare Tillich's attitude to the use of the Bible in Christian theology with Barth's (see Vol. 1, pp. 67 ff). The Bible is a *normative* source for Christian theology, certainly, but this does not mean that one can read off theology deductively from the Bible. For one thing the Bible does not provide the terms for an inclusive systematized theology. For another theology has to take account of the experience of a believing community like the Church. On the shelf, the Bible is not a witness to anything; it only functions in the life of the Church. Furthermore the theologian's use of the Bible needs to be related to his use of culture in general.]

If the task of systematic theology is to explain the contents of the Christian faith, three questions immediately arise: What are the sources of systematic theology? What is the medium of their reception? What is the norm determining the use of the sources? The first answer to these questions might be the Bible. The Bible is the original document about the events on which Christianity is based. Although this cannot be denied, the answer is insufficient. In dealing with the question of the sources of systematic theology, we must reject the assertion of neo-orthodox biblicism[1] that the Bible is the *only* source. The biblical message cannot be understood and could not have been received had there been no preparation for it in human religion and culture. And the biblical message would not have become a message for anyone, including the theologian himself, without the experiencing participation of the Church and of every Christian. If the 'Word of God' or the 'act of revelation' is called the source of systematic theology, it must be emphasized that the 'Word of God' is not limited to the words of a book and that the act of revelation is not the 'inspiring' of a 'book of revelations', even if the book is the document of the final 'Word of God', the fulfilment and criterion of all revelations. The biblical message embraces more (and less) than the biblical books. Systematic theology, therefore, has additional sources beyond the Bible.

The Bible, however, is the basic source of systematic theology because it is the original document about the events on which the Christian Church is founded. If we use the word 'document' for the Bible, we must exclude legal connotations. The Bible is not a legally conceived, formulated, and sealed record about a divine 'deed' on the basis of which claims can be decided. The documentary character of the Bible is identical with the fact that it contains the original witness of those who participated in the revealing events. Their participation was their response to the happenings which became revealing events through this response. The inspiration of the biblical writers is their receptive and creative response to potentially revelatory facts. The inspiration of the writers of the New Testament is their acceptance of Jesus as the Christ, and with him, of the New Being, of which they became witnesses. Since there is no revelation unless there is someone who receives it as revelation, the act of reception is a part of the event itself.

[1] Tillich here has Barth in mind (Ed.).

The Bible is both original event and original document; it witnesses to that of which it is a part.

The biblical material as a source of systematic theology is presented in a methodological way by the historical theologian. Biblical theology, in co-operation with the other disciplines of historical theology, opens the Bible as the basic source of systematic theology. But how it does this is by no means obvious. The biblical theologian, to the degree to which he is a theologian (which includes a systematic point of view), does not present pure facts to us; he gives us theologically interpreted facts. His exegesis is pneumatic (spiritual) or, as we should call it today, 'existential'. He speaks of the results of his philosophical and detached interpretation as matters of ultimate concern to him. He unites philology and devotion in dealing with the biblical texts. It is not easy to do this with fairness to both points of view. A comparison of any recent scientific commentary on Romans (e.g., C. H. Dodd or Sanday and Headlam[1]) with Barth's pneumatic-existential interpretation of it lays bare the unbridged gap between both methods. All theologians, and especially the students of systematic theology, suffer because of this situation. Systematic theology needs a biblical theology which is historical-critical without any restrictions and, at the same time, devotional-interpretative, taking account of the fact that it deals with matters of ultimate concern. It is possible to fulfil this demand, for that which concerns us ultimately is not linked with any special conclusion of historical and philological research. A theology which is dependent on predetermined results of the historical approach is bound to something conditional which claims to be unconditional, that is, with something demonic. And the demonic character of any demand imposed on the historian for definite results becomes visible in the fact that it destroys his honesty. Being ultimately concerned about what is really ultimate liberates the theologian from all 'sacred dishonesty'. It makes conservative as well as revolutionary historical criticism open to him. Only such free historical work, united with the attitude

[1] C. H. Dodd, *The Epistle to the Romans*, ?—??—? (Fontana Books); W. Sanday and A. C. Headlam, *A Critical and Exegetical Commentary on the Epistle to the Romans*, 1895, International Critical Commentary (Ed.).

of ultimate concern, can open the Bible to the systematic theologian as his basic source.

The genesis of the Bible is an event in Church history—an event in a comparatively late stage of early Church history. The systematic theologian, therefore, in using the Bible as a source, implicitly uses Church history as a source. He must do this explicitly. Systematic theology has a direct and definite relation to Church history. On this point there is a real difference between the Catholic and the Protestant attitude, and no systematic theologian can escape a decision about it. The decision is easy for those who are bound by the authority of the Roman Church. It is also easy for those who believe that Protestantism means a radical biblicism and who assume that radical biblicism is a possible theological position. But most theologians in the non-Roman Churches are not willing to accept this alternative. It is obvious to them that the radical biblicistic attitude is a self-deception. No one is able to leap over two thousand years of Church history and become contemporaneous with the writers of the New Testament, except in the Spiritual sense of accepting Jesus as the Christ. Every person who encounters a biblical text is guided in his religious understanding of it by the understanding of all previous generations. Even the Reformers were dependent on the Roman tradition against which they protested. They directed special elements of the ecclesiastical tradition against others in order to fight the distortion which had affected the whole tradition, but they did not and could not jump out of the tradition into the situation of Matthew and Paul. The Reformers were aware of this situation, and their orthodox systematisers were still aware of it. Evangelical biblicism, both past and present, is unaware of it, and produces a 'biblical' theology which actually is dependent on definite dogmatic developments of the post-Reformation period. Through historical scholarship the difference between the dogmatic teaching of most American evangelical churches and the original meaning of the biblical texts can easily be shown. Church history cannot be evaded; therefore, it is a religious as well as a scholarly necessity that the relationship of systematic theology to the ecclesiastical tradition be stated frankly and pointedly.

Another approach which is not acceptable to most non-Roman theologians is the subjection of systematic theology to the decisions of councils and popes. Roman Catholic dogmatics uses those doctrinal traditions which have gained legal standing (*de fide*) as the real source of systematic theology. It presupposes dogmatically, with or without *a posteriori* proofs, that those doctrines whose validity is guaranteed by canon law agree essentially with the biblical message. The work of the systematic theologian is an exact and, at the same time, polemic interpretation of the statements *de fide*. This is the reason for the dogmatic sterility of Roman Catholic theology, in contrast to its liturgical and ethical creativity and the great scholarship it develops in areas of Church history which are free from dogmatic prohibitions. It is important for the ecumenical character of systematic theology that Greek Orthodox theologians, although they accept the authority of tradition, deny the legalization of tradition by papal authority. This gives the Greek Orthodox theologian creative possibilities from which Roman theologians are excluded. Protestant theology protests in the name of the Protestant principle against the identification of our ultimate concern with any creation of the Church, including the biblical writings in so far as their witness to what is really ultimate concern is also a conditioned expression of their own spirituality. Therefore, it is able to use all the materials provided by Church history. It can make use of Greek and Roman and German and modern concepts in interpreting the biblical message; it can make use of the decisions of sectarian protests against official theology; but it is not bound to any of these concepts and decisions.

A special problem arises from the fact that no one is actually able to handle all these materials, because the denominational structures operate as an unconscious and conscious principle of selection. This cannot be avoided, and it has a creative side. The ecclesiastical and theological climate in which the theologian grows up or for which he has later made a personal decision produces understanding through familiarity. Without such familiarity no existential use of the Church-historical material is possible. The systematic theologian encounters in the concrete life of his denomination in its liturgy and hymns, its sermons and sacraments, that which concerns him ultimately—the New Being in Jesus as the Christ. Therefore, the denominational tradition is a decisive source for the systematic theologian, however ecumenically he may use it.

The biblical source is made available to the systematic theologian through a critical and ultimately concerned biblical theology. In the same way Church history is made available to the systematic theologian through a historically critical and ultimately concerned history of Christian thought, formerly called 'history of dogma'. The traditional term 'dogmatics' implies a concern which the more recent term does not express. The 'history of Christian thought' can mean a detached description of the ideas of theological thinkers through the centuries. Some of the critical histories of Christian thought are not far removed from such an attitude. The historical theologian must show that in all periods Christian thought has dealt with matters of ultimate concern and that therefore it is itself a matter ol ultimate concern. Systematic theology needs a history of Christian thought written from a point of view which is radically critical and, at the same time, existentially concerned.

A broader source of systematic theology than all those mentioned so far is the material presented by the history of religion and culture. Its impact on the systematic theologian begins with the language he uses and the cultural education he has received. His spiritual life is shaped by his social and individual encounter with reality. This is expressed in the language, poetry, philosophy, religion, etc., of the cultural tradition in which he has grown up and from which he takes some content in every moment of his life, in his theological work and also outside it. Beyond this immediate and unavoidable contact with his culture and religion, the systematic theologian deals with them directly in many ways. He uses culture and religion intentionally as his means of expression, he points to them for confirmation of his statements, he fights against them as contradictions of the Christian message, and, above all, he formulates the existential questions implied in them, to which his theology intends to be the answer.

This continuous and never ending use of cultural and religious contents as a source of systematic theology raises the question: How are these contents made available for use in a way parallel to the method by which the biblical theologian makes the biblical materials available and the historian of Christian thought makes the doctrinal materials available? There is no established answer to this question, since neither a theological history of religion nor a theological history of culture has been theoretically conceived and practically established.

A theological history of religion should interpret theologically the material produced by the investigation and analysis of the pre-religious and religious life of mankind. It should elaborate the motives and types of religious expression, showing how they follow from the nature of the religious concern and therefore necessarily appear in all religions, including Christianity in so far as it is a religion. A theological history of religion also should point out demonic distortions and new tendencies in the religions of the world, pointing to the Christian solution and preparing the way for the acceptance of the Christian message by the adherents of non-Christian religions. One could say that a theological history of religion should be carried through in the light of the missionary principle that the New Being in Jesus as the Christ is the answer to the question asked implicitly and explicitly by the religions of mankind. Some materials taken from a theological history of religion appear in the present theological system.

A theological history of culture cannot be a continuous historical report (this is also true of the theological history of religion). It can only be what I like to call a 'theology of culture',[1] which is the attempt to analyse the theology behind all cultural expressions, to discover the ultimate concern in the ground of a philosophy, a political system, an artistic style, a set of ethical or social principles. This task is analytic rather than synthetic, historical rather than systematic. It is a preparation for the work of the systematic theologian. At the present time a theology of culture is continuously being constructed from the non-theological, and, less vigorously, from the theological side. It has become an important part of the many critical analyses of the present world situation, of the cultural

---

[1] Paul Tillich, 'Uber die Idee einer Theologie der Kultur', in *Kanstudien* (Berlin: Pan-Verlag, Rolf Heise, 1920); see also my *The Religious Situation* (New York: Henry Holt and Co., 1932).

decline of the West, of developments in special realms. Theological analysis has been carried on in connection with the history of modern thought, art, science, social movements (called in German *Geistesgeschichte*, 'the history or spiritual life'). It should, however, be worked out in a more organized way by theologians. It should be taught as 'the theology of culture' in all institutions of theological learning; for instance, as theological history of philosophy, the arts, etc. Concerning the method of such a theological analysis of culture the following might be said. The key to the theological understanding of a cultural creation is its style. Style is a term derived from the realm of the arts, but it can be applied to all realms of culture. There is a style of thought, of politics, of social life, etc. The style of a period expresses itself in its cultural forms, in its choice of objects, in the attitudes of its creative personalities, in its institutions and customs. It is an art as much as a science to 'read styles', and it requires religious intuition, on the basis of an ultimate concern, to look into the depth of a style, to penetrate to the level where an ultimate concern exercises its driving power. This, however, is what is demanded of the theological historian of culture, and in performing this function he opens up a creative source for systematic theology.

(FROM : *Systematic Theology*, I, pp. 39–45.)

2 THE EXISTENCE OF GOD

[Tillich here discusses belief in the existence of God and uses the term 'being' to do it. We can start from our ordinary use of the phrase 'human beings' for ourselves, by which we refer to our existence as separate individuals. By analogy theology has made use of the phrase 'divine being' of God, and this has often given the impression that God is to be thought of as also a separate Being, however perfect, over against finite human beings. Tillich is anxious to emphasize that God exists in a way so incommensurate with our being that strictly speaking one has to say that God does not exist—in the way human beings exist. Nevertheless their existence as 'beings' is derived from God's 'Being'—he is the cause of their effect—so that it might be better for us to think of our being, our existence, in God. We all participate in being, and it is this fact which gives their peculiar potency and effectiveness to symbols.]

The being of God is being-itself. The being of God cannot be understood as the existence of a being alongside others or above others. If God is *a* being he is subject to the categories of finitude, especially to space and substance. Even if he is called the 'highest being' in the sense of the 'most perfect' and the 'most powerful' being, this situation is not changed. When applied to God, superlatives become diminutives. They place him on the level of other beings while elevating him above all of them. Many theologians who have used the term 'highest being' have known better. Actually they have described the highest as the absolute, as that which is on a level qualitatively different from the level of any being—even the highest being. Whenever infinite or unconditional power and meaning are attributed to the highest being, it has ceased to be *a* being and has become being-itself. Many confusions in the doctrine of God and many apologetic weaknesses could be avoided if God were understood first of all as being-itself or as the ground of being. The power of being is another way of expressing the same thing in a circumscribing phrase. Ever since the time of Plato it has been known—although it often has been disregarded, especially by the nominalists[1] and their modern followers—that the concept of being as being, or being-itself, points to the power inherent in everything, the power of resisting non-being. Therefore, instead of saying that God is first of all being-itself, it is possible to say that he is the power of being in everything and above everything, the infinite power of being. A theology which does not dare to identify God and the power of being as the first step toward a doctrine of God relapses into monarchic monotheism, for if God is not being-itself he is subordinate to it, just as Zeus is subordinate to fate in Greek religion. The structure of being-itself is his fate, as it is the fate of all other beings. But God is his own fate; he is 'by himself'; he possesses 'aseity'.[2] This can be said of him only if he is the power of being, if he is being-itself.

As being-itself God is beyond the contrast of essential and existential being. We have spoken of the transition of being into existence, which involves the possibility that being will contradict and lose itself. This transition is excluded from being-itself (except in terms of the Christological paradox), for being-itself does not participate in non-being. In this it stands in contrast to every being. As classical theology has emphasized, God is beyond essence and existence. Logically, being-itself is 'before', 'prior to', the split which characterizes finite being.

For this reason it is as wrong to speak of God as the universal essence as it is to speak of him as existing. If God is understood as universal essence, as the form of all forms, he is identified with the unity and totality of finite potentialities; but he has ceased to be the power of the ground in all of them, and therefore he has ceased to transcend them. He has poured all his creative power into a system of forms, and he is bound to these forms. This is what pantheism means.

On the other hand, grave difficulties attend the attempt to speak of God as existing. In order to maintain the truth that

[1] From Latin *nominalis* ('belonging to a name'). The nominalists taught that abstract terms, like ' Being ' as Tillich uses it, did not relate to anything that really existed but were mere words. (Ed.)

[2] Self-sufficient being in himself, in no way dependent on anything outside himself. (Ed.)

God is beyond essence and existence while simultaneously arguing for the existence of God, Thomas Aquinas is forced to distinguish between two kinds of divine existence: that which is identical with essence and that which is not. But an existence of God which is not united with its essence is a contradiction in terms. It makes God a being whose existence does not fulfil his essential potentialities; being and not-yet-being are 'mixed' in him, as they are in everything finite. God ceases to be God, the ground of being and meaning. What really has happened is that Thomas has had to unite two different traditions: the Augustinian, in which the divine existence is included in his essence, and the Aristotelian, which derives the existence of God from the existence of the world and which then asserts, in a second step, that his existence is identical with his essence. Thus the question of the existence of God can be neither asked nor answered. If asked, it is a question about that which by its very nature is above existence, and therefore the answer—whether negative or affirmative—implicitly denies the nature of God. It is as atheistic to affirm the existence of God as to deny it. God is being-itself, not *a* being. On this basis a first step can be taken toward the solution of the problem which usually is discussed as the immanence and the transcendence of God. As the power of being, God transcends every being and also the totality of being—the world. Being-itself is beyond finitude and infinity; otherwise it would be conditioned by something other than itself, and the real power of being would lie beyond both it and that which conditioned it. Being-itself infinitely transcends every finite being. There is no proportion or gradation between the finite and the infinite. There is an absolute break, an infinite 'jump'. On the other hand, everything finite participates in being-itself and in its infinity. Otherwise it would not have the power of being. It would be swallowed by non-being, or it never would have emerged out of non-being. This double relation of all beings to being-itself gives being-itself a double characteristic. In calling it creative we point to the fact that everything participates in the infinite power of being. In calling it abysmal we point to the fact that everything participates in the power of being in a finite way, that all beings are infinitely transcended by their creative ground.

Man is bound to the categories of finitude. He uses the two categories of relation—causality and substance—to express the relation of being-itself to finite beings. The 'ground' can be interpreted in both ways, as the cause of finite beings and as their substance. The former has been elaborated by Leibniz[1] in the line of the Thomistic tradition, and the latter has been elaborated by Spinoza[2] in the line of the mystical tradition. Both ways are impossible. Spinoza establishes a naturalistic pantheism, in contrast to the idealistic type which identifies God with the universal essence of being, which denies finite freedom and in so doing denies the freedom of God. By necessity God is merged into the finite beings, and their being is his being. Here again it must be emphasized that pantheism does not say that God is everything. It says that God is the substance of everything and that there is no substantial independence and freedom in anything finite.

Therefore, Christianity, which asserts finite freedom in man and spontaneity in the non-human realm, has rejected the category of substance in favour of the category of causality in attempting to express the relation of the power of being to the beings who participate in it. Causality seems to make the world dependent on God, and, at the same time, to separate God from the world in the way a cause is separated from its effect. But the category of causality cannot 'fill the bill', for cause and effect are not separate; they include each other and form a series which is endless in both directions. What is cause at one point in this series is effect at another point and conversely. God as cause is drawn into this series, which drives even him beyond himself. In order to disengage the divine cause from the series of causes and effects, it is called the first cause, the absolute beginning. What this means is that the category of causality is being denied while it is being used. In other words, causality is being used not as a category but as a symbol. And if this is done and is understood the difference between substance and causality disappears, for if God is the cause of the entire series of causes and effects, he is the substance underlying the whole process of becoming. But this 'underlying' does not have the character of a substance

---

[1] Gottfried Wilhelm Leibniz (1646–1716), German philosopher. (Ed.)
[2] Baruch Spinoza (1632–77), Dutch Jewish philosopher. (Ed.)

which underlies its accidents and which is completely expressed by them. It is an underlying in which substance and accidents preserve their freedom. In other words, it is substance not as a category but as a symbol. And, if taken symbolically there is no difference between *prima causa* and *ultima substantia*. Both mean what can be called in a more directly symbolic term 'the creative and abysmal ground of being'. In this term both naturalistic pantheism, based on the category of substance, and rationalistic theism, based on the category of causality, are overcome.

Since God is the ground of being, he is the ground of the structure of being. He is not subject to this structure; the structure is grounded in him. He *is* this structure, and it is impossible to speak about him except in terms of this structure. God must be approached cognitively through the structural elements of being-itself. These elements make him a living God, a God who can be man's concrete concern. They enable us to use symbols which we are certain point to the ground of reality.

(FROM : *Systematic Theology*, I, pp. 261–4.)

3 FAITH AS ULTIMATE CONCERN

[In this passage Tillich makes his famous definition of religious faith as 'ultimate concern'. When asked by a student to clarify the meaning of this term he said 'taking something with ultimate seriousness' (*Ultimate Concern,* p. 7). Tillich means by the term more than that which may be, as we say, a matter of life and death to us. It is more too than deciding what to us is most important in life. It has this subjective quality but it is also objective in that it involves the sense of being shown, being made aware, that nature or the arts or science or moral endeavour point coercively to an abiding reality.]

We have used the term 'ultimate concern' without explanation. Ultimate concern is the abstract translation of the great commandment: 'The God, our God, the Lord is one; and you shall love the Lord your God with all your heart, and with all your soul, and with all your mind, and with all your strength' (Mark 12:29 R.S.V.). The religious concern is ultimate; it excludes all other concerns from ultimate significance; it makes them preliminary. The ultimate concern is unconditional, independent of any conditions of character, desire, or circumstance. The unconditional concern is total: no part of ourselves or of our world is excluded from it; there is no 'place' to flee from it (Psalm 139). The total concern is infinite: no moment of relaxation and rest is possible in the face of a religious concern which is ultimate, unconditional, total and infinite.

The word 'concern' points to the 'existential' character of religious experience. We cannot speak adequately of the 'object of religion' without simultaneously removing its character as an object. That which is ultimate gives itself only to the attitude of ultimate concern. It is the correlate of an unconditional concern but not a 'highest thing' called 'the absolute' or 'the unconditioned', about which we could argue in detached objectivity. It is the object of total surrender, demanding also the surrender of our subjectivity while we look at it. It is a matter of infinite passion and interest (Kierkegaard), making us its object whenever we try to make it our object. For this reason we have avoided terms like '*the* ultimate', '*the* unconditioned', '*the* universal', '*the* infinite' and have spoken of ultimate, unconditional, total, infinite concern. Of course, in every concern there is *something* about which one is concerned; but this something should not appear as a separated object which could be known and handled without concern. This, then, is the first formal criterion of theology: *The object of theology is what concerns us ultimately. Only those propositions are theological which deal with their object in so far as it can become a matter of ultimate concern for us.*

The negative meaning of this proposition is obvious. Theology should never leave the situation of ultimate concern and try to play a role within the arena of preliminary concerns. Theology cannot and should not give judgements about the aesthetic value of an artistic creation, about the scientific value of a physical theory or a historical conjecture, about the best methods of medical healing or social reconstruction, about the solution of political or international conflicts. The theologian *as* theologian is no expert in any matters of preliminary concern. And, conversely, those who are experts in these matters should not *as such* claim to be experts in theology. The first formal principle of theology, guarding the boundary line between ultimate concern and preliminary concerns, protests theology as well as the cultural realms on the other side of the line.

But this is not its entire meaning. Although it does not indicate the content of the ultimate concern and its relation to the preliminary concerns, it has implications in both respects. There are three possible relations of the preliminary concerns to that which concerns us ultimately. The first is mutual indifference, the second is a relation in which a preliminary concern is elevated to ultimacy, and the third is one in which a preliminary concern becomes the vehicle of the ultimate concern without claiming ultimacy for itself. The first relation is predominant in ordinary life with its oscillation between conditional, partial, finite situations and experiences and moments when the question of the ultimate meaning of existence takes hold of us. Such a division, however, contradicts the unconditional, total and infinite character of the religious concern. It places our ultimate concern beside other concerns and deprives it of its ultimacy. This attitude sidesteps the ultimacy of the biblical commandments and that of the first theological criterion. The second relation is idolatrous in its very nature. Idolatry is the elevation of a preliminary concern to ultimacy. Something essentially conditioned is taken as unconditional, something essentially partial is boosted into universality, and something essentially finite is given infinite significance (the best example is the contemporary idolatry of religious nationalism). The conflict between the finite basis of such a concern and its infinite claim leads to a conflict of ultimates; it radically contradicts the biblical commandments and the first theological criterion. The third relation between the ultimate concern and the preliminary concerns makes the latter bearers and vehicles of the former. That which is a finite concern is not elevated to infinite significance, nor is it put beside the infinite, but in and through it the infinite becomes real. Nothing is excluded from this function. In and through every preliminary concern the ultimate concern can actualize itself. Whenever this happens, the preliminary concern becomes a possible object of theology. But theology deals with it only in so far as it is a medium, a vehicle, pointing beyond itself.

Pictures, poems, and music can become objects of theology, not from the point of view of their aesthetic form, but from the point of view of their power of expressing some aspects of that which concerns us ultimately, in and through their aesthetic form. Physical or historical or psychological insights can become objects of theology, not from the point of view of their cognitive form, but from the point of view of their power of revealing some aspects of that which concerns us ultimately in and through their cognitive form. Social ideas and actions, legal projects and procedures, political programmes and decisions, can become objects of theology, not from the point of view of their social, legal, and political form, but from the point of view of their power of actualizing some aspects of that which concerns us ultimately in and through their social, legal, and political forms. Personality problems and developments, educational aims and methods, bodily and mental healing, can become objects of theology, not from the point of view of their ethical and technical form, but from the point of view of their power of mediating some aspects of that which concerns us ultimately in and through their ethical and technical form.

The question now arises: What is the content of our ultimate concern? What *does* concern us conditionally? The answer, obviously, cannot be a special object, not even God, for the first criterion of theology must remain formal and general. If more is to be said about the nature of our ultimate concern, it must be derived from an analysis of the concept 'ultimate concern'. *Our ultimate concern is that which determines our being or non-being. Only those statements are theological which deal with their object in so far as it can become a matter of being or non-being for us.* This is the second formal criterion of theology.

Nothing can be of ultimate concern for us which does not have the power of threatening and saving our being. The term 'being' in this context does not designate existence in time and space. Existence is continuously threatened and saved by things and events which have no ultimate concern for us. But the term 'being' means the whole of human reality, the structure, the meaning, and the aim of existence. All this is threatened; it can be lost or saved. Man is ultimately concerned about his being and meaning. 'To be or not to be' in *this* sense is a matter of ultimate unconditional total, and infinite concern. Man is infinitely concerned about the infinity to which he belongs, from which he is separated, and for which he is longing. Man is totally concerned about the totality which is his true being and which is disrupted in time and space. Man is unconditionally concerned about that which conditions his being beyond all the conditions in him and around him. Man is ultimately concerned about that which determines his ultimate destiny beyond all preliminary necessities and accidents.

The second formal criterion of theology does not point to any special content, symbol, or doctrine. It remains formal and, consequently, open for contents which are able to express 'that which determines our being or non-being'. At the same time it excludes contents which do not have this power from entering the theological realm. Whether it is a god who is a being beside others (even a highest being) or an angel who inhabits a celestial realm (called the realm of 'spirits') or a man who possesses supernatural powers (even if he is called a god-man)—none of these is an object of theology if it fails to withstand the criticism of the second formal criterion of theology, that is, if it is not a matter of being or non-being for us.

(FROM: *Systematic Theology*, I, pp. 14–18.)

4 THE HISTORICAL JESUS AND BELIEF IN CHRIST

[Tillich is here concerned with the crucial problem of the place of the historical Jesus in Christian belief. To what extent does the historical Jesus matter? Tillich sketches the problems of reconstructing, on the base of the findings of historical criticism, a 'Life of Jesus'. He then criticizes two common reactions to the inconclusive results of 'The quest of the historical Jesus'. One is to say that what really matters is the ethical teaching of Jesus and this can be separated from the question of belief about his person. This is the approach of the 'liberal protestantism' of people like Adolf von Harnack. The other reaction is to say that the essence of the teaching of Jesus, his 'message', is about the necessity for 'decision'. Here Tillich has in mind existentialist theologians like Bultmann. Tillich then hints generally at his own approach which would be to say that the teaching of Jesus is inseparable from his person and that everything turns on what one believes he was and did (including his teaching on this): 'The cross is the symbol of a gift before it is the symbol of a demand'.]

From the moment that the scientific method of historical research was applied to biblical literature, theological problems which were never completely absent became intensified in a way unknown to former periods of Church history. The historical method unites analytical-critical and constructive-conjectural elements. For the average Christian consciousness shaped by the orthodox doctrine of verbal inspiration, the first element was much more impressive than the second. One felt only the negative element in the term 'criticism' and called the whole enterprise 'historical criticism' or 'higher criticism', or, with reference to a recent method, 'form criticism'. In itself the term 'historical criticism' means nothing more than historical research. Every historical research criticizes its sources, separating what has more probability from that which has less or is altogether improbable. Nobody doubts the validity of this method, since it is confirmed continuously by its success; and nobody seriously protests if it destroys beautiful legends and deeply rooted prejudices. But biblical research became suspect from its very beginning. It seemed to criticize not only the historical sources but the revelation contained in these sources. Historical research and rejection of biblical authority were identified. Revelation, it was implied, covered not only the revelatory content but also the historical form in which it had appeared. This seemed to be especially true of the facts concerning the 'historical Jesus'. Since the biblical revelation is essentially historical, it appeared to be impossible to separate the revelatory content from the historical reports as they are given in the biblical records. Historical criticism seemed to undercut faith itself.

But the critical part of historical research into biblical literature is the less important part. More important is the constructive-conjectural part, which was the driving force in the whole enterprise. The facts behind the records, especially the facts about Jesus, were sought. There was an urgent desire to discover the reality of this man, Jesus of Nazareth, behind the colouring and covering traditions which are almost as old as the reality itself. So the research for the so-called 'historical Jesus' started. Its motives were religious and scientific at the same time. The attempt was courageous, noble and extremely significant in many respects. Its theological consequences are numerous and rather important. But, seen in the light of its basic intention, the attempt of historical criticism to find the empirical truth about Jesus of Nazareth was a failure. The historical Jesus, namely, the Jesus behind the symbols of his reception as the Christ, not only did not appear but receded farther and farther with every new step. The history of the attempts to write a 'life of Jesus' elaborated by Albert Schweitzer in his early work, *The Quest of the Historical Jesus*, is still valid. His own constructive attempt has been corrected. Scholars, whether conservative or radical, have become more cautious, but the methodological situation has not changed. This became manifest when R. Bultmann's bold programme of a 'demythologization of the New Testament' [1] aroused a storm in all theological camps and the slumber of Barthianism with respect to the historical problem was followed by an

---

[1] See Vol. 2, pp. 64 ff.

astonished awakening. But the result of the new (and very old) questioning is not a picture of the so-called historical Jesus but the insight that there is no picture behind the biblical one which could be made scientifically probable.

This situation is not a matter of a preliminary shortcoming of historical research which will some day be overcome. It is caused by the nature of the sources itself. The reports about Jesus of Nazareth are those of Jesus as the Christ, given by persons who had received him as the Christ. Therefore, if one tries to find the real Jesus behind the picture of Jesus as the Christ, it is necessary critically to separate the elements which belong to the factual side of the event from the elements which belong to the receiving side. In doing so, one sketches a 'Life of Jesus'; and innumerable such sketches have been made. In many of them scientific honesty, loving devotion, and theological interest have worked together. In others critical detachment and even malevolent rejection are visible. But none can claim to be a probable picture which is the result of the tremendous scientific toil dedicated to this task for two hundred years. At best, they are more or less probable results, able to be the basis neither of an acceptance nor of a rejection of the Christian faith.

In view of this situation, there have been attempts to reduce the picture of the historical Jesus to the 'essentials', to elaborate a *Gestalt*[1] while leaving the particulars open to doubt. But this is not a way out. Historical research cannot paint an essential picture after all the particular traits have been eliminated because they are questionable. It remains dependent on the particulars. Consequently, the pictures of the historical Jesus in which the forms of a 'Life of Jesus' is wisely avoided still differ from one another as much as those in which such self-restriction is not applied.

The dependence of the *Gestalt* on the valuation of the particulars is evident in an example taken from the complex of what Jesus thought about himself. In order to elaborate this point, one must know, besides many other things, whether he applied the title 'Son of Man' to himself and, if so, in what sense. Every answer given to this question is a more or less probable hypothesis, but the character of the 'essential' picture

---

[1] *Gestalt*: general picture. (Ed.)

of the historical Jesus depends decisively on this hypothesis. Such an example clearly shows the impossibility of replacing the attempt to portray a 'Life of Jesus' by trying to paint the '*Gestalt* of Jesus'.

At the same time, this example shows another important point. People who are not familiar with the methodological side of historical research and are afraid of its consequences for Christian doctrine like to attack historical research generally and the research in the biblical literature especially, as being theologically prejudiced. If they are consistent, they will not deny that their own interpretation is also prejudiced or, as they would say, dependent on the truth of their faith. But they deny that the historical method has objective scientific criteria. Such an assertion, however, cannot be maintained in view of the immense historical material which has been discovered and often empirically verified by a universally used method of research. It is characteristic of this method that it tries to maintain a permanent self-criticism in order to liberate itself from any conscious or unconscious prejudice. This is never completely successful, but it is a powerful weapon and necessary for achieving historical knowledge.

One of the examples often given in this context is the treatment of the New Testament miracles. The historical method approaches the miracle stories neither with the assumption that they have happened because they are attributed to him who is called the Christ nor with the assumption that they have not happened because such events would contradict the laws of nature. The historical method asks how trustworthy the records are in every particular case, how dependent they are on older sources, how much they might be influenced by the credulity of a period, how well confirmed they are by other independent sources, in what style they are written, and for what purpose they are used in the whole context. All these questions can be answered in an 'objective' way without necessary interference of negative or positive prejudices. The historian never can reach certainty in this way, but he can reach high degrees of probability. It would, however, be a leap to another level if he transformed historical probability into positive or negative historical certainty by a judgement of faith (as will be shown at a later point). This clear distinction is often confused by the obvious fact that the understanding of the meaning of a text is partly dependent on the categories of understanding used in the encounter with texts and records. But it is not wholly dependent on them, since there are philological as well as other aspects which are open to an objective approach. Understanding demands one's participation in what one understands, and we can participate only in terms of what we are, including our own categories of understanding. But this 'existential' understanding should never prejudice the judgement of the historian concerning facts and relations. The person whose ultimate concern is the content of the biblical message is in the same position as the one who is indifferent to it if such questions are discussed as the development of the Synoptic tradition, or the mythological and legendary elements of the New Testament. Both have the same criteria of historical probability and must use them with the same rigour, although doing so may affect their own religious or philosophical convictions or prejudices. In this process, it may happen that prejudices which close the eyes to particular facts open them to others. But this 'opening of the eyes' is a personal experience which cannot be made into a methodological principle. There is only one methodological procedure, and that is to look at the subject matter and not at one's own looking at the subject matter. Actually, such looking is determined by many psychological, sociological, and historical factors. These aspects must be neglected intentionally by everyone who approaches a fact objectively. One must not formulate a judgement about the self-consciousness of Jesus from the fact that one is a Christian—or an anti-Christian. It must be derived from a degree of plausibility based on records and their probable historical validity. This, of course, presupposes that the content of the Christian faith is independent of this judgement.

The search for the historical Jesus was an attempt to discover a minimum of reliable facts about the man Jesus of Nazareth, in order to provide a safe foundation for the Christian faith. This attempt was a failure. Historical research provided probabilities about Jesus of a higher or lower degree. On the basis of these probabilities, it sketched 'Lives of Jesus'. But they were more like novels than biographies, they certainly could not provide a safe foundation for the Christian faith. Christianity is not based on the acceptance of a historical novel; it is based on the witness to the messianic character of Jesus by people who were not interested at all in a biography of the Messiah.

The insight into this situation induced some theologians to give up any attempt to construct a 'life' or a *Gestalt* of the historical Jesus and to restrict themselves to an interpretation of the 'words of Jesus'. Most of these words (though not all of them) do not refer to himself and can be separated from any biographical context. Therefore, their meaning is independent of the fact that he may or may not have said them. On that basis the insoluble biographical problem has no bearing on the truth of the words rightly or wrongly recorded as the words of Jesus. That most of the words of Jesus have parallels in contemporaneous Jewish literature is not an argument against their validity. This is not even an argument against their uniqueness and power as they appear in collections like the Sermon on the Mount, the parables, and the discussions with foes and followers alike.[1]

A theology which tries to make the words of Jesus into the historical foundation of the Christian faith can do so in two ways. It can treat the words of Jesus as the 'teachings of Jesus' or as the 'message of Jesus'. As the teachings of Jesus, they are understood as refined interpretations of the natural law or as original insights into the nature of man. They have no relation to the concrete situation in which they are spoken. As such, they belong to the law, prophecy, or Wisdom literature such as is found in the Old Testament. They may transcend all three categories in terms of depth and power; but they do not transcend them in terms of character. The retreat in historical research to the 'teachings of Jesus' reduces Jesus to the level of the Old Testament and implicitly denies his claim to have overcome the Old Testament context.

The second way in which historical research restricts itself to the words of Jesus is more profound than the first. It denies

[1] This refers also to the discovery of the Dead Sea Scrolls, which—in spite of much sensationalism in the publicity given to it—has opened the eyes of many people to the problem of biblical research but which has not changed the theological situation at all.

that the words of Jesus are general rules of human behaviour, that they are rules to which one has to subject one's self, or that they are universal and can therefore be abstracted from the situation in which they were spoken. Instead, they emphasize Jesus' message that the Kingdom of God is 'at hand' and that those who want to enter it must decide for or against the Kingdom of God. These words of Jesus are not general rules but concrete demands. This interpretation of the historical Jesus, suggested especially by Rudolf Bultmann, identifies the meaning of Jesus with that of his message. He calls for a decision, namely, the decision for God. And this decision includes the acceptance of the Cross, by his own acceptance of the Cross. The historically impossible, namely, to sketch a 'life' of a *Gestalt* of Jesus, is ingeniously avoided by using the immediately given—namely, his message about the Kingdom of God and its conditions—and by keeping as nearly as possible to the 'paradox of the Cross of Christ'. But even this method of restricted historical judgement cannot give a foundation to the Christian faith. It does not show how the requirement of deciding for the Kingdom of God can be fulfilled. The situation of having to decide remains one of being under the law. It does not transcend the Old Testament situation, the situation of the quest for the Christ. One could call this theology 'existentialist liberalism' in contrast to the 'legalist liberalism' of the first. But neither method can answer the question of wherein lies the power to obey the teachings of Jesus or to make the decision for the Kingdom of God. This these methods cannot do because the answer must come from a new reality, which, according to the Christian message, is the New Being in Jesus as the Christ. The Cross is the symbol of a gift before it is the symbol of a demand. But, if this is accepted, it is impossible to retreat from the being of the Christ to his words. The last avenue of the search for the historical Jesus is barred, and the failure of the attempt to give a foundation to the Christian faith through historical research becomes obvious.

This result would probably have been more easily acknowledged if it had not been for the semantic confusion about the meaning of the term 'historical Jesus'. The term was predominantly used for the results of historical research into the character and life of the person who stands behind the Gospel reports. Like all historical knowledge, our knowledge of this person is fragmentary and hypothetical. Historical research subjects this knowledge to methodological scepticism and to continuous change in particulars as well as essentials. Its ideal is to reach a high degree of probability, but in many cases this is impossible.

The term 'historical Jesus' is also used to mean that the event 'Jesus as the Christ' has a factual element. The term in this sense raises the question of faith and not the question of historical research. If the factual element in the Christian event were denied, the foundation of Christianity would be denied. Methodological scepticism about the work of historical research does not deny this element. Faith cannot even guarantee the name 'Jesus' in respect to him who was the Christ. It must leave that to the incertitudes of our historical knowledge. But faith does guarantee the factual transformation of reality in that personal life which the New Testament expresses in its picture of Jesus as the Christ. No fruitful and honest discussion is possible if these two meanings of the term 'historical Jesus' are not clearly distinguished.

(FROM: *Systematic Theology*, II, pp. 116–23.)

5 THE CROSS AND RESURRECTION OF CHRIST

[The crucifixion and the resurrection of Christ test the realism of the Christian's belief. Because the Incarnation was real it meant participating in the whole reach of the human tragic experience including death. As genuine history the crucifixion can be mistaken for 'one more tragic event'. Similarly the resurrection is a real conquest of life over death, although it can be taken as only a vulgar wonder-story.

The resurrection is an ambiguous sign to faith and not an indisputable event that can be established by some historical reconstruction. There have been attempts at the latter like the stories of the empty tomb, or the suggestion that the resurrection means the survival of the soul of Jesus, or finally the idea that it relates only to some interior experience of the disciples. Tillich then presents his own 'restitution-theory'. His meaning is very elusive, and readers will find it useful to ponder whether this presentation of the resurrection as the continuing power of the Christ as the New Being is essentially any different from Bultmann's treatment (see Vol. 2, pp. 70ff.)]

The 'Cross of the Christ' and the 'Resurrection of the Christ' are interdependent symbols; they cannot be separated without losing their meaning. The Cross of the Christ is the Cross of the one who has conquered the death of existential estrangement. Otherwise it would only be one more tragic event (which it *also* is) in the long history of the tragedy of man. And the Resurrection of the Christ is the Resurrection of the one who, as the Christ, subjected himself to the death of existential estrangement. Otherwise it would be only one more questionable miracle story (which it also is in the records).

If Cross and Resurrection are interdependent, they must be both reality and symbol. In both cases something happened within existence. Otherwise the Christ would not have entered existence and could not have conquered it. But there is a qualitative difference. While the stories of the Cross probably point to an event that took place in the full light of historical observation, the stories of the Resurrection spread a veil of deep mystery over the event. The one is a highly probable fact; the other a mysterious experience of a few. One can ask whether this qualitative difference does not make a real inter-dependence impossible? Is it perhaps wiser to follow the suggestion of those scholars who understand the Resurrection as a symbolic interpretation of the Cross without any kind of objective reality?[1]

The New Testament lays tremendous significance on the objective side of the Resurrection; at the same time, it elevates the objective event indicated in the stories of the Crucifixion to universal symbolic significance. One could say that in the minds of the disciples and of the writers of the New Testament the Cross is both an event and a symbol and that the Resurrection is both a symbol and an event. Certainly, the Cross of Jesus is seen as an event that happened in time and space. But, as the Cross of the Jesus who is the Christ, it is a symbol and a part of a myth. It is the myth of the bearer of the new eon who suffers the death of a convict and slave under the powers of that old eon which he is to conquer. This Cross, whatever the historical circumstances may have been, is a symbol based on a fact.

But the same is true of the Resurrection. The resurrection of gods and half-gods is a familiar mythological symbol. It plays a major role in some mystery cults in which mystical participation in the death and the resurrection of the god on the part of the initiated is the ritual centre. A belief in the future resurrection of the martyrs grew up in later Judaism. In the moment in which Jesus was called the Christ and the combination of his messianic dignity with an ignominious death was asserted—whether in expectation or in retrospec-tion—the application of the idea of resurrection to the Christ was almost unavoidable. The disciples' assertion that the symbol had become an event was dependent in part upon their belief in Jesus, who, as the Christ, became the Messiah. But it was affirmed in a way which transcended the mythological symbolism of the mystery cults, just as the concrete picture of Jesus as the Christ transcended the mythical pictures of the

[1] Tillich has Bultmann in mind, see Vol. 2, pp. 73 ff. (Ed.)

mystery gods. The character of this event remains in darkness, even in the poetic rationalization of the Easter story. But one thing is obvious. In the days in which the certainty of his Resurrection grasped the small, dispersed, and despairing group of his followers, the Church was born, and, since the Christ is not the Christ without the Church, he has become the Christ. The certainty that he who is the bringer of the new eon cannot finally have succumbed to the powers of the old eon made the experience of the Resurrection the decisive test of the Christ-character of Jesus of Nazareth. A real experience made it possible for the disciples to apply the known symbol of resurrection to Jesus, thus acknowledging him definitely as the Christ. They called this experienced event the 'Resurrection of the Christ', and it was a combination of event and symbol.

The attempt has been made to describe both events, the Cross and the Resurrection, as factual events separated from their symbolic meaning. This is justified, in so far as the significance of both symbols rests on the combination of symbol and fact. Without the factual element, the Christ would not have participated in existence and consequently not have been the Christ. But the desire to isolate the factual from the symbolic element is, as has been shown before, not a primary interest of faith. The results of the research for the purely factual element can never be on the basis of faith or theology.

With this in mind, one can say that the historical event underlying the Crucifixion story shines with comparative clarity through the different and often contradictory legendary reports. Those who regard the passion story as cult-legend, which is told in various ways, simply agree with the thesis presented about the symbolic character of the Cross of the Jesus who is the Christ. The only factual element in it having the immediate certainty of faith is the surrender of him who is called the Christ to the ultimate consequence of existence, namely, death under the conditions of estrangement. Everything else is a matter of historical probability, elaborated out of legendary interpretation.

The event which underlies the symbol of the Resurrection must be treated in an analogous way. The factual element is a necessary implication of the symbol of the Resurrection (as it is of the symbol of the Cross). Historical research is justified in trying to elaborate this factual element on the basis of the legendary and mythological material which surrounds it. But historical research can never give more than a probable answer. The faith in the Resurrection of the Christ is neither positively nor negatively dependent on it. Faith can give certainty only to the victory of the Christ over the ultimate consequence of the existential estrangement to which he subjected himself. And faith can give this certainty because it is itself based on it. Faith is based on the experience of being grasped by the power of the New Being through which the destructive consequences of estrangement are conquered.

It is the certainty of one's own victory over the death of existential estrangement which creates the certainty of the Resurrection of the Christ as event and symbol; but it is not historical conviction or the acceptance of biblical authority which creates this certainty. Beyond this point there is no certainty but only probability, often very low, sometimes rather high.

There are three theories which try to make the event of the Resurrection probable. The most primitive theory, and at the same time most beautifully expressed, is the physical one. It is told in the story of the tomb which the women found empty on Easter morning. The sources of this story are rather late and questionable, and there is no indication of it in the earliest tradition concerning the event of the Resurrection, namely, 1 Corinthians, chapter 15. Theologically speaking, it is a rationalization of the event, interpreting it with physical categories that identify resurrection with the presence or absence of a physical body. Then the absurd question arises as to what happened to the molecules which comprise the corpse of Jesus of Nazareth. Then absurdity becomes compounded into blasphemy.

A second attempt to penetrate into the factual side of the Resurrection event is the spiritualistic one. It uses, above all, the appearances of the Resurrected as recorded by Paul. It explains them as manifestations of the soul of the man Jesus to his followers, in analogy to the self-manifestations of the souls of the dead in spiritualistic experiences. Obviously, this is not the Resurrection of the Christ but an attempt to prove the general immortality of the soul and the claim that it has the general ability after death to manifest itself to the living. Spiritualistic experiences may or may not be valid. But, even if valid, they cannot explain the factual side of the Resurrection of the Christ symbolized as the reapparance of the total personality, which includes the bodily expression of his being. This is so much the case that he can be recognized in a way which is more than the manifestation of a bodiless 'spirit'.

The third attempt to approach the factual side of the Resurrection is the psychological one. It is the easiest and most accepted way of describing the factual element in the Resurrection. Resurrection is an inner event in the minds of Jesus' adherents. Paul's description of the Resurrection experiences (including his own) lends itself to the psychological interpretation. And—if we exclude the physical interpretation—Paul's words, like the story of his conversion, point to something which happened in the minds of those who had the experiences. This does not imply that the event itself was 'merely' psychological, namely, wholly dependent on psychological factors in the minds of those whom Paul enumerates (e.g., an intensification of the memory of Jesus). But the psychological theory misses the reality of the event which is presupposed in the symbol—the event of the Resurrection of the Christ.

The preceding theory concerning the event which underlies the symbol of Resurrection dismisses physical as well as spiritualistic literalism. It replaces both by a description which keeps nearer to the oldest source (1 Cor., chap. 15) and which places at the centre of its analysis the religious meaning of the Resurrection for the disciples (and all their followers), in contrast to their previous state of negativity and despair. This view is the ecstatic confirmation of the indestructible unity of the New Being and its bearer, Jesus of Nazareth. In eternity they belong together. In contrast to the physical, the spiritualistic, and the psychological theories concerning the Resurrection event, one could call this the 'restitution theory'. According to it, the Resurrection is the restitution of Jesus as the Christ, a restitution which is rooted in the personal unity between Jesus and God and in the impact of this unity on the minds of the apostles. Historically, it may well be that the restitution of Jesus to the dignity of the Christ in the minds of the disciples may precede the story of the acceptance of Jesus as the Christ by Peter. The latter may be a reflex of the former; but, even if this is the case, the experience of the New Being in Jesus must precede the experience of the Resurrected.

Although it is my conviction that the restitution theory is most adequate to the facts, it must also be considered a theory. It remains in the realm of probability and does not have the certainty of faith. Faith provides the certainty that the picture of the Christ in the Gospels is a personal life in which the New Being has appeared in its fullness and that the death of Jesus of Nazareth was not able to separate the New Being from the picture of its bearer. If physical or spiritualistic literalists are not satisfied with this solution, they cannot be forced to accept it in the name of faith. But they can perhaps grant that the attitude of the New Testament and especially of the non-literalistic Apostle Paul justifies the theory of restitution.

(FROM: *Systematic Theology*, II, pp. 176–82.)

FOR FURTHER STUDY AND DISCUSSION

1 Theology and religion are often taken to be the same thing. How would you distinguish them? Is religious belief necessary for the study of theology?

2 Is the use of paradox, metaphor and symbol necessary in religious language? How would you distinguish poetic language from religious language?

3 What are the advantages and disadvantages of thinking of God in terms of 'Being'? Can you suggest a better category?

4 How does Tillich's approach to the Bible compare with Barth's?

5 Compare Tillich and Bultmann on the meaning of the resurrection of Christ.

6 'One is tempted to say that for Tillich the meaning of Christian belief is exhausted in the present attitude and experience of the believer' (H. A. Meynell). Is it true to say that Tillich tends to dissolve the content of faith into our subjective attitudes to it?

FOR FURTHER READING

PRINCIPAL WORKS OF PAUL TILLICH

The Protestant Era, London, 1957.
The Courage to be, London (Fontana Books), 1962.
The New Being, London, 1956.
The Shaking of the Foundations, London (Pelican Books), 1962.
The Eternal Now, Sermons, London, 1963.
Morality and Beyond, London, 1964.
Systematic Theology, London, Vol. I 1953, Vol. II 1957, Vol. III 1964.
Theology of Culture, New York (Galaxy Books), 1964.
Ultimate Concern: Tillich in dialogue, London, 1965 (useful for Tillich's clarifications of some of the obscurities in his *Systematic Theology*).

SOME BOOKS ABOUT PAUL TILLICH

Charles W. Kegley and Robert W. Bretall (Eds.), *The theology of Paul Tillich*, London, 1952. (A volume of essays by theologians and philosophers on various aspects of Tillich's thought, with a chapter of autobiography and replies to criticisms by Tillich himself.)
Walter Leibrecht (Ed.), *Religion and culture*: essays in honour of Paul Tillich, London, 1959.
G. H. Tavard, *Paul Tillich and the Christian message*, London, 1962. (An examination of Tillich's theology by a Roman Catholic theologian.)
J. Heywood Thomas, *Paul Tillich*: an appraisal, London, 1963.
A. J. McElway, *The Systematic Theology of Paul Tillich*: a review and analysis, London, 1964 (an exposition of the contents of the three volumes of Tillich's *Systematic Theology*).

FOR GENERAL BACKGROUND READING

John Macquarrie, *Twentieth-century Religious Thought*, 1963.
——, *God-talk*, 1967.
——, *God and Secularity*, 1968.
Frederick Ferré, *Language, Logic and God*, 1962.
——, *Basic Modern Philosophy of Religion*, 1968.
David E. Jenkins, *Guide to the Debate about God*, 1966.
Colin Williams, *Faith in a Secular Age*, 1966.
E. L. Mascall, *The Secularisation of Christianity*, 1965.
H. Gollwitzer, *The Existence of God as confessed by faith*, 1964.
A. M. Ramsey, *God, Christ and the World*, 1969.
T. W. Ogletree, *The Death of God Controversy*, 1966.